Peterborough Ontario and Area in Photos, Saving Our History One Photo at a Time

Photography
by Barbara Raué
2012

Series Name:
Cruising Ontario

Book 29: Peterborough and Area

Cover photo: Peterborough Armouries,
220 Murray Street, Peterborough

Series Name: Cruising Ontario

Book 1: London
Book 2: Dundas
Book 3: Hamilton
Book 4: Oakville
Book 5: Chesley
Book 6: Stoney Creek
Book 7: Waterdown
Book 8: Owen Sound
Book 9: Mount Forest
Book 10: Dundalk
Book 11: Burford and Area
Book 12: Waterford and Area
Book 13: Drumbo and Area
Book 14: Sheffield and Area
Book 15: Tavistock and Area
Book 16: Ancaster and Mount Hope
Book 17: Innerkip
Book 18: Brantford
Book 19: Burlington
Book 20: Guelph and Area
Book 21: Ayr
Book 22: Erin
Book 23: Goderich
Book 24: Lucknow
Book 25: Orangeville and Area
Book 26: Toronto
Book 27: Beaver Valley
Book 28: Collingwood
Book 29: Peterborough and Area

Other Books by Barbara Raue

Coins of Gold

Arrows, Indians and Love

The Life and Times of Barbara
Volume 1: Inventions That Have Enhanced My Life
Volume 2: Entertainment That I Have Enjoyed
Volume 3: East Coast Trips
Volume 4: Olympics
Volume 5: Wonders of the World
Volume 6: Caribbean Cruises
Volume 7: Animals
Volume 8: Storms and Other Major Disasters in My Lifetime
Volume 9: Wars, Terrorist Attacks, Major Disasters

Peterborough

Peterborough is a city on the Otonabee River in central Ontario, 125 kilometres (78 miles) northeast of Toronto. Peterborough's nickname of "The Electric City" underscores the historical and present day importance of technology and manufacturing as an economic base of the city which has operations from large multi-national companies such as Seimans, Rolls Royce, and General Electric. Peterborough is known as the gateway to the Kawarthas, "cottage country", a large recreational region of the province. In 1818, Adam Scott settled on the west shore of the Otonabee River and the following year he began construction of a sawmill and gristmill, establishing the area as Scott's Plains. The mill was located at the foot of present-day King Street and was powered by water from Jackson Creek.

The year 1825 marked the arrival of 1,878 Irish immigrants from the city of Cork, a British Parliament experimental emigration plan to transport poor Irish families to Upper Canada. The scheme was managed by Peter Robinson, a politician in York (present-day Toronto). Scott's Plains was renamed Peterborough in his honour. The Irish emigrated from the Emerald Isle to escape over-crowding, poverty, political unrest, religious tensions, disease and the potato famine. By 1851 almost half of the town of Peterborough claimed Irish ancestry. They cleared the land in the rolling hills of the Peterborough countryside

In 1845, Sandford Fleming, inventor of Standard Time and designer of Canada's first postage stamp, moved to the city to live with Dr. John Hutchison and his family, staying until 1847. Dr. John Hutchison was one of Peterborough's first resident doctors.

Beginning in the late 1850s, a canoe building industry grew up in and around Peterborough. The Peterborough Canoe Company was founded in 1893, with the factory being built on the site of the original Adam Scott mill. From 1928–36 the Johnson Motor Company/Outboard Marine (the makers of motorized boat engines) was established as an outgrowth of the original industry.

Peterborough was one of the first places in the country to begin generating hydro electrical power (even before the plants at Niagara Falls). Companies like Edison General Electric Company (later Canadian General Electric) and America Cereal Company (later to become Quaker Oats, and in 2001 PepsiCo, Inc.), opened to take advantage of cheap hydro-electric power.

Bridgenorth

Bridgenorth is located on Chemong Lake in the Kawarthas. It is located north of Peterborough on Chemong Road.

Emerald Isle

Emerald Isle is located on Buckhorn Lake.

Ennismore

Ennismore is located in Selwyn Township in central-eastern Ontario.

Peterborough

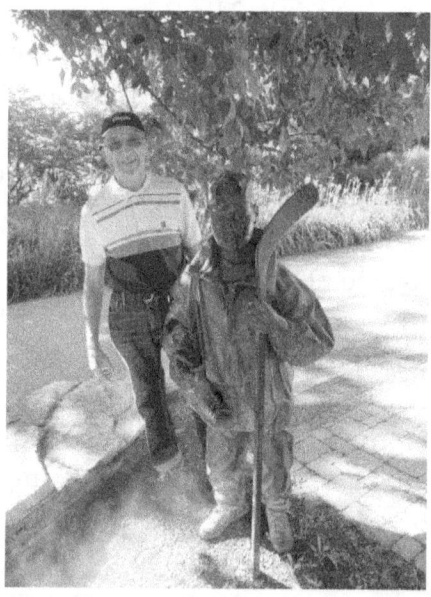

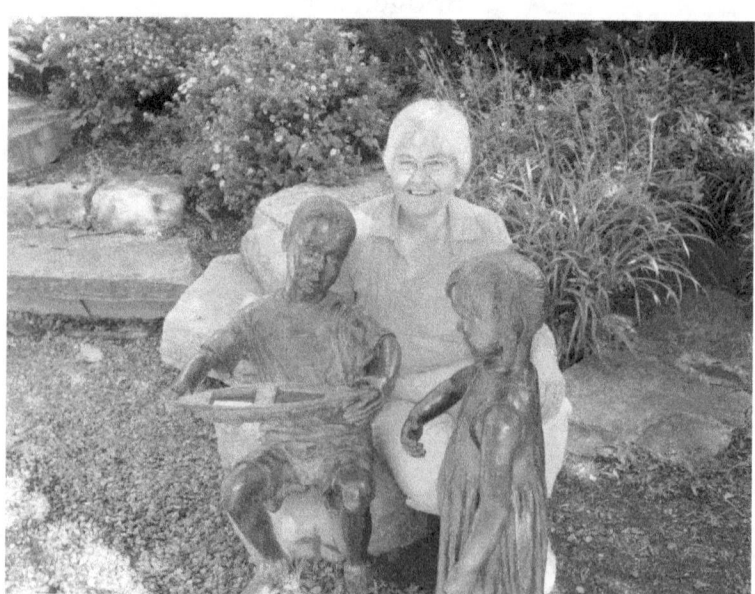

Boat Launching by Laura Brown Breetvelt

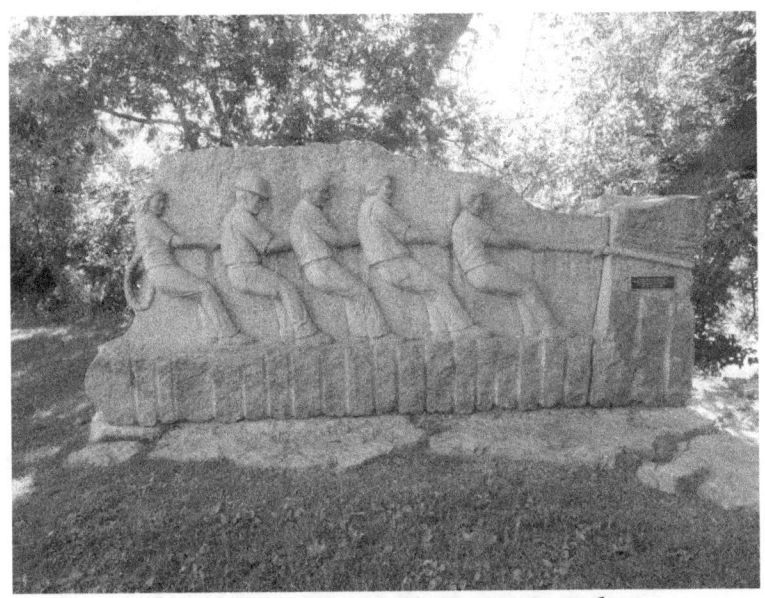

Dedicated to men and women workers
past, present and future

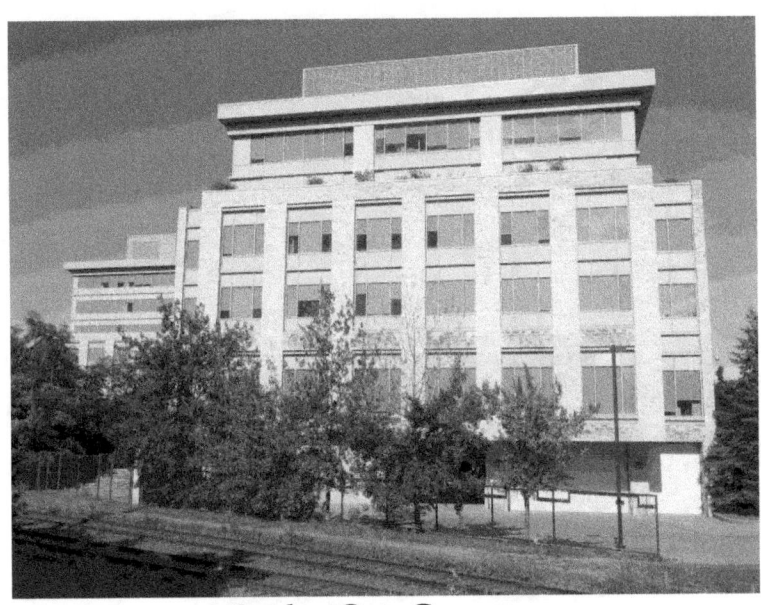

Quaker Oats Company

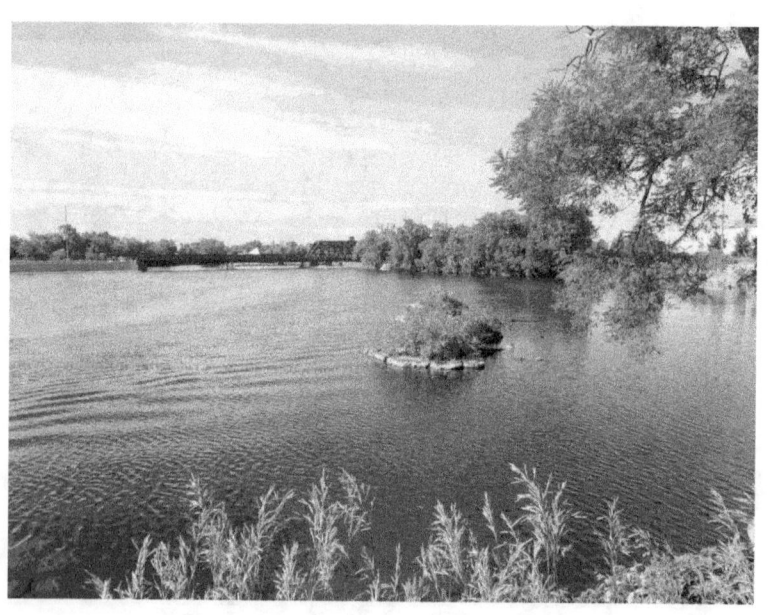

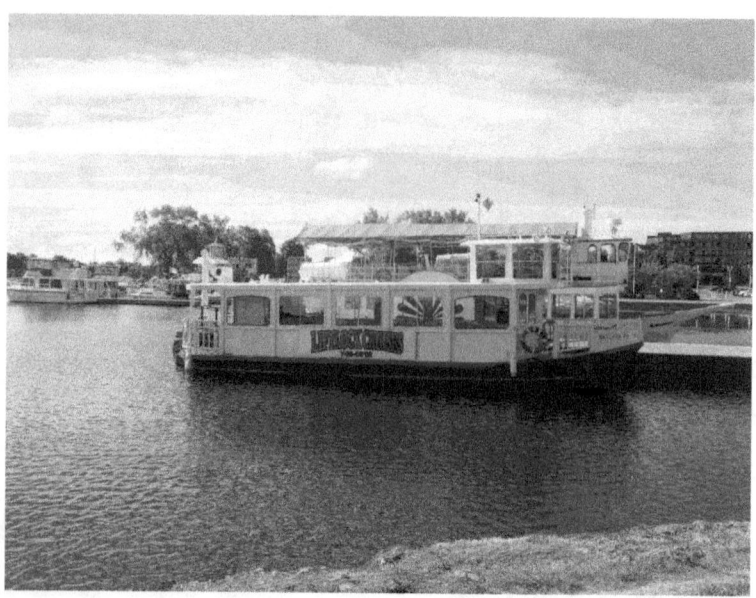

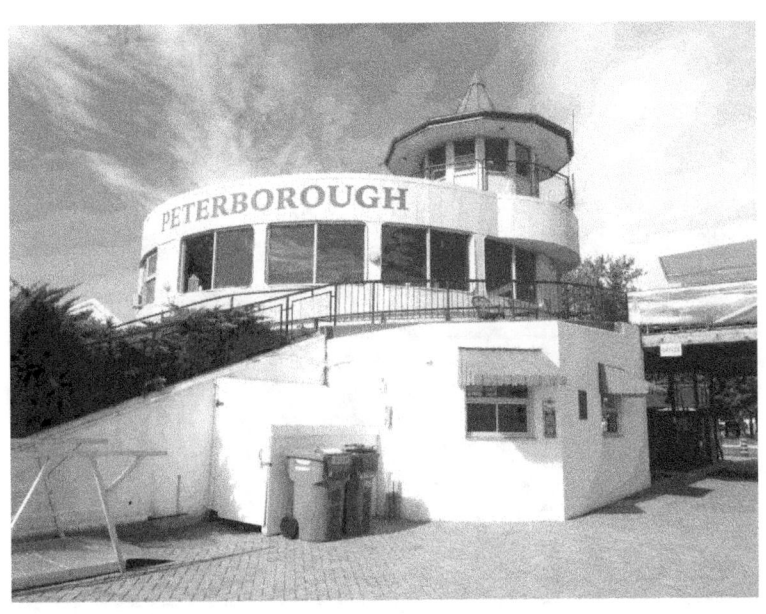

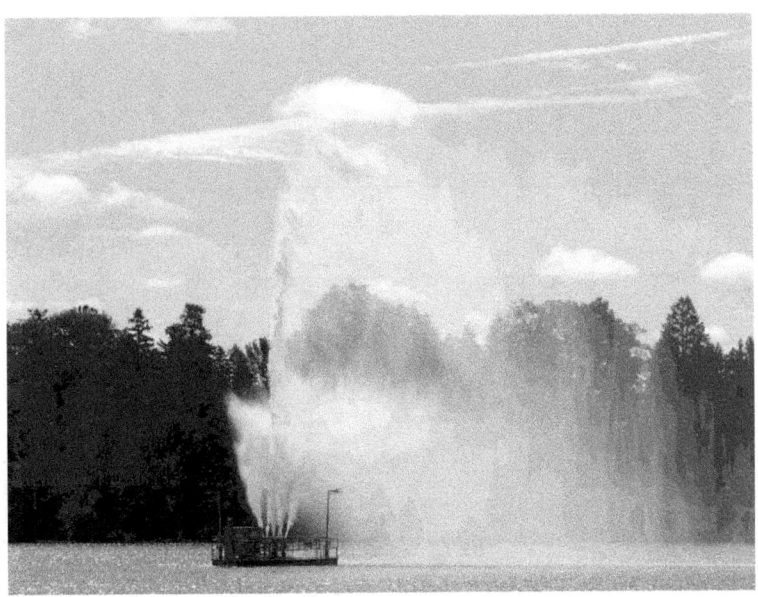

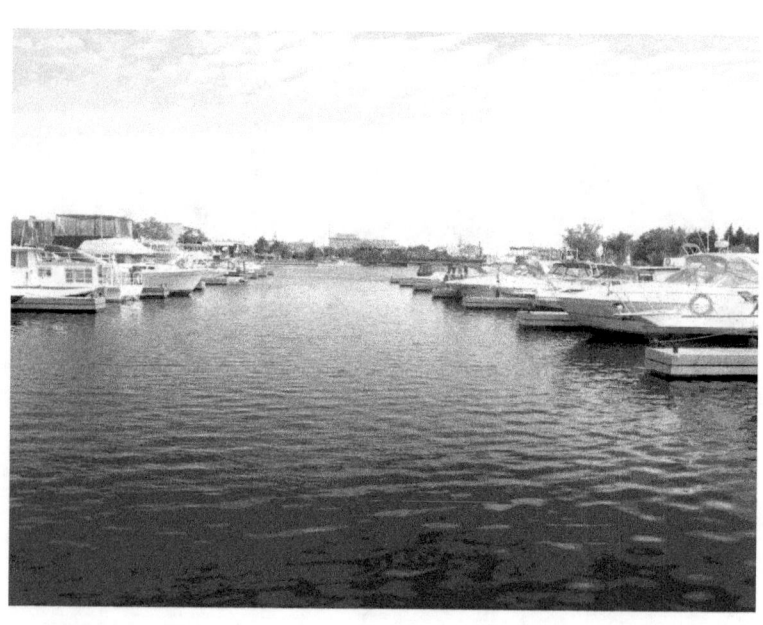

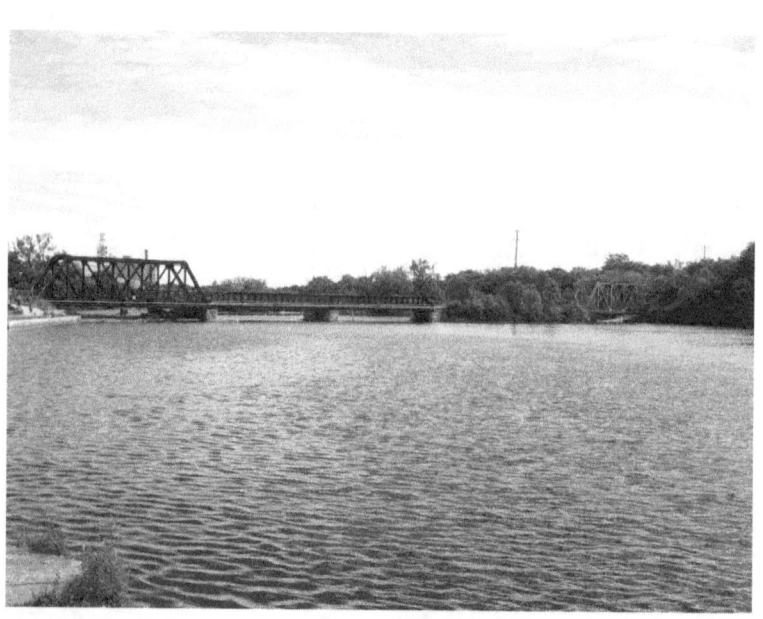

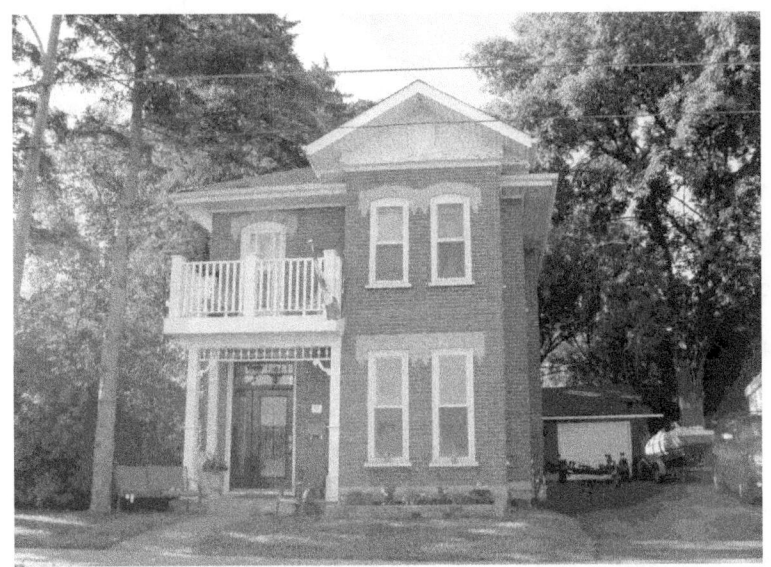

#45

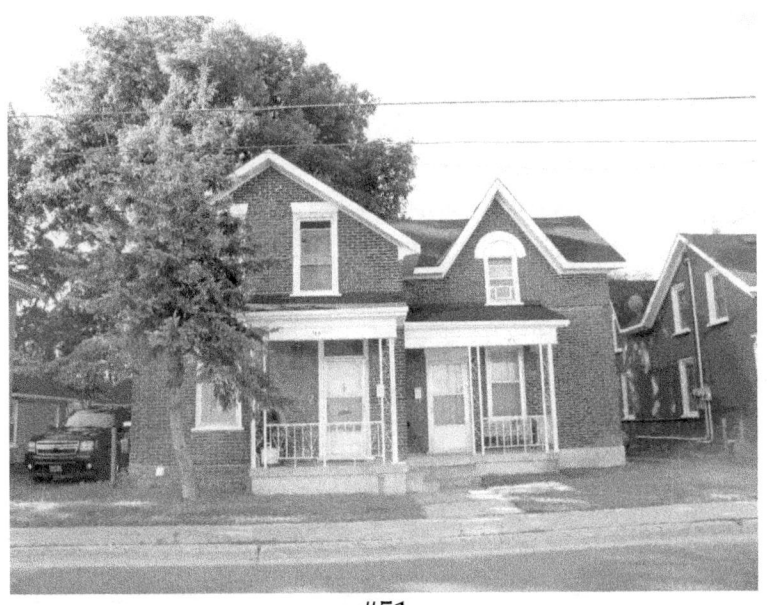

#51

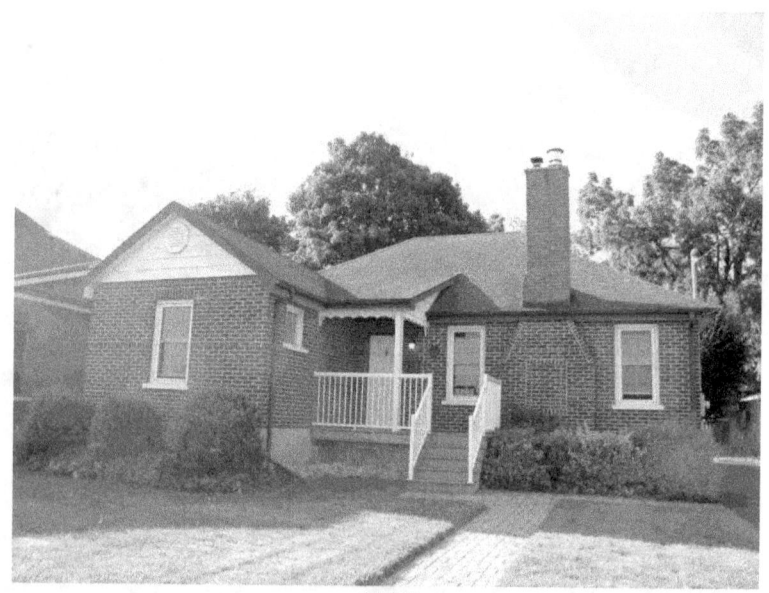

#105

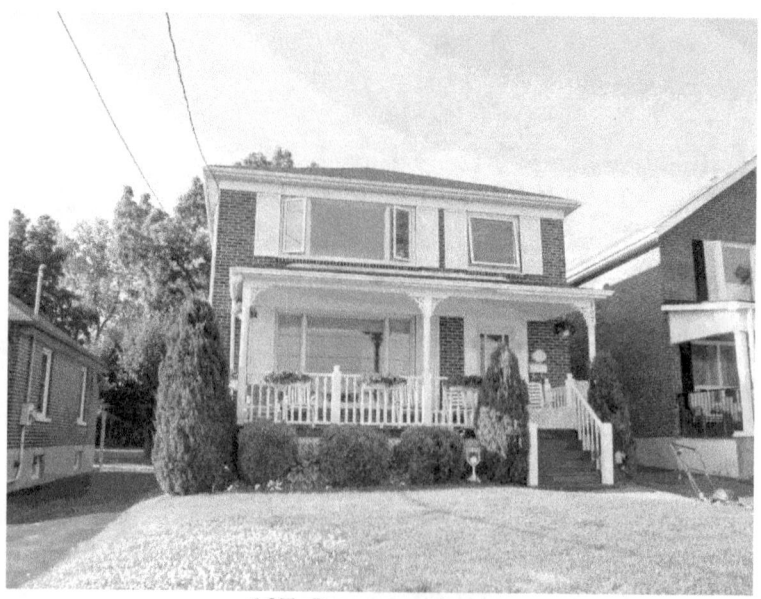

107 Crescent Street

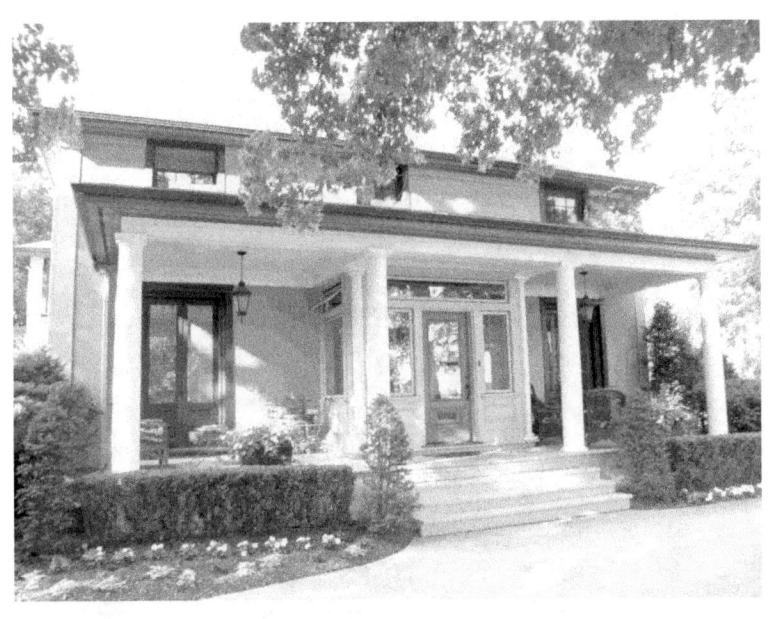

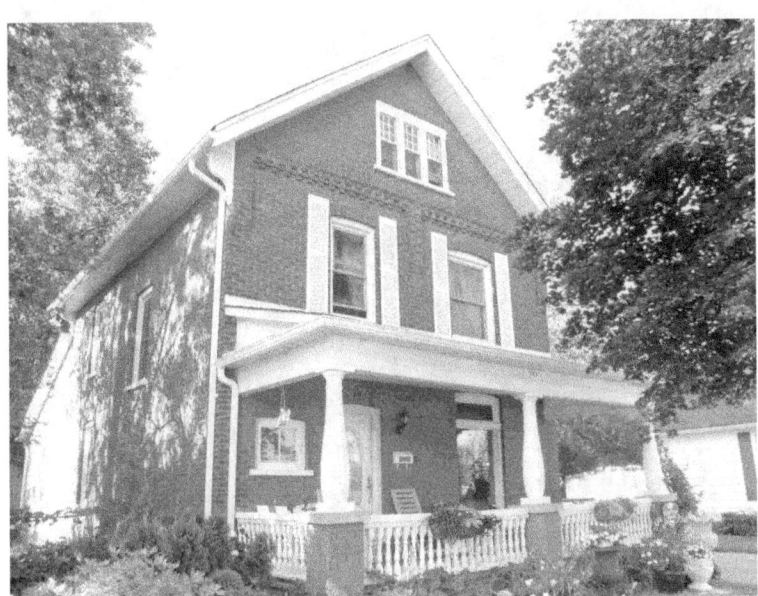

147 Crescent Street

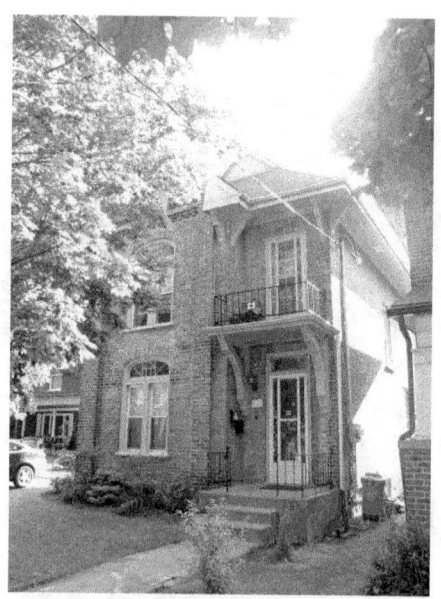

120 Crescent Street

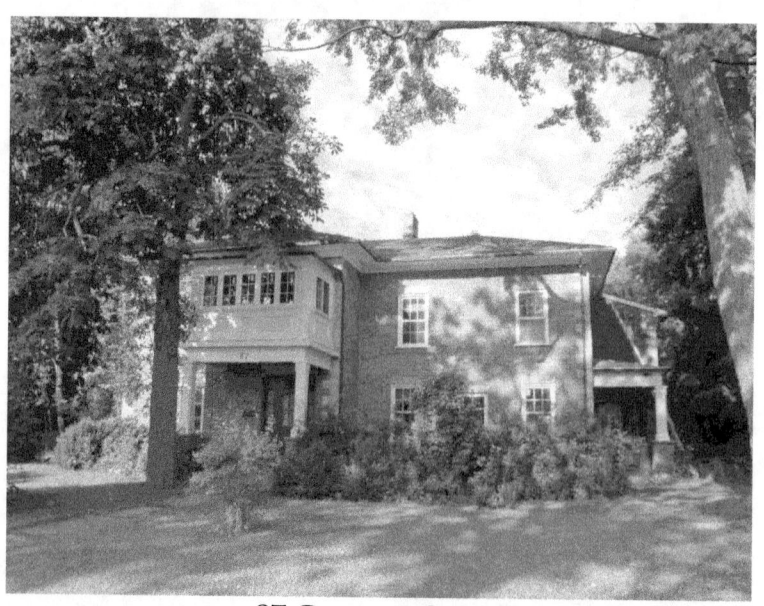

87 Crescent Street

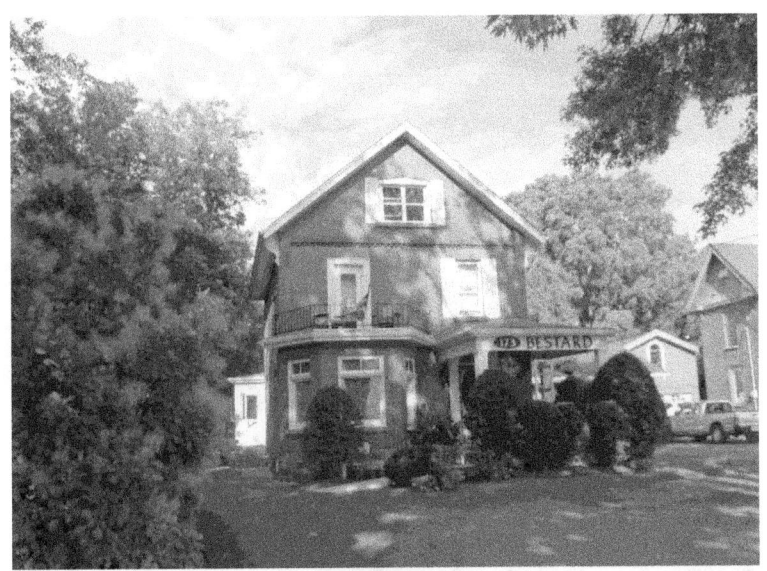

173 Bestard

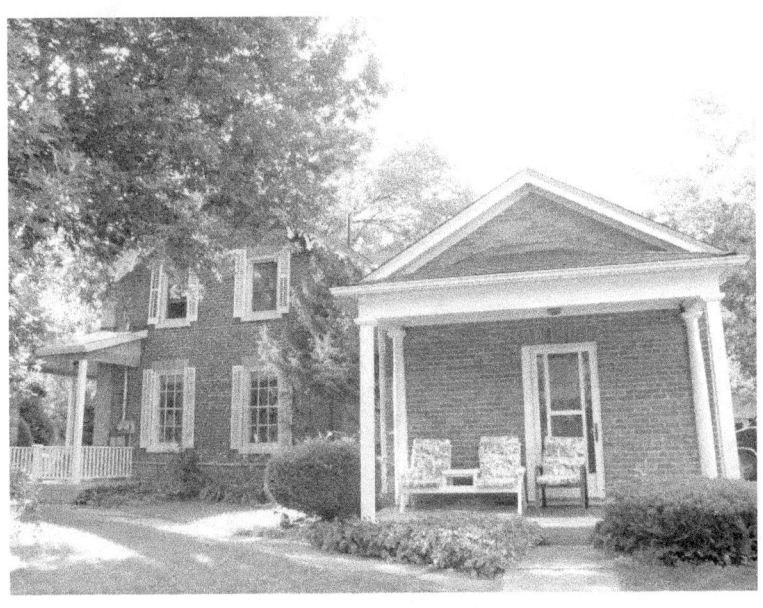

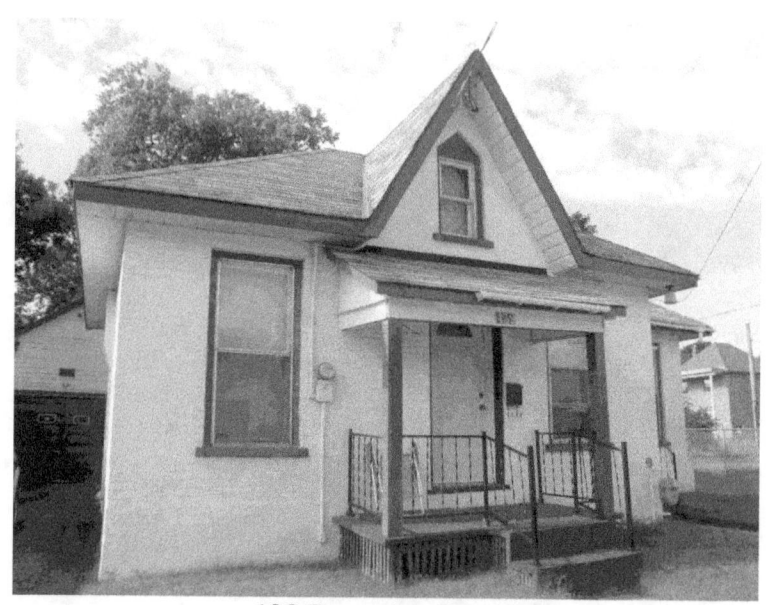

139 Romaine Street

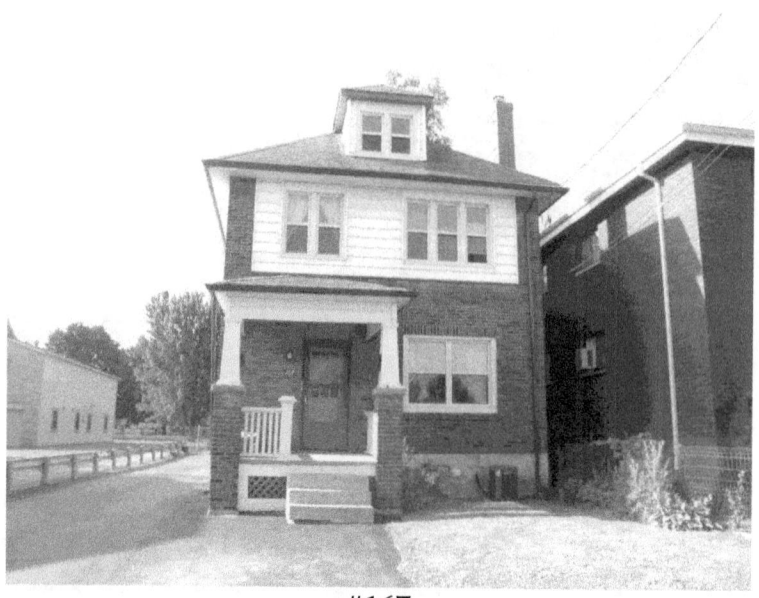

#167

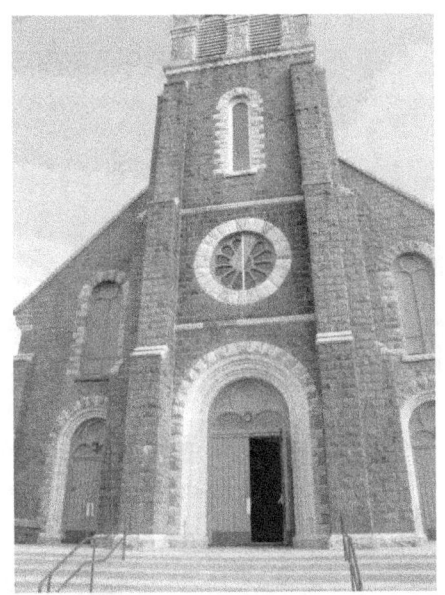

Sacred Heart of Jesus founded 1909
208 Romaine Street

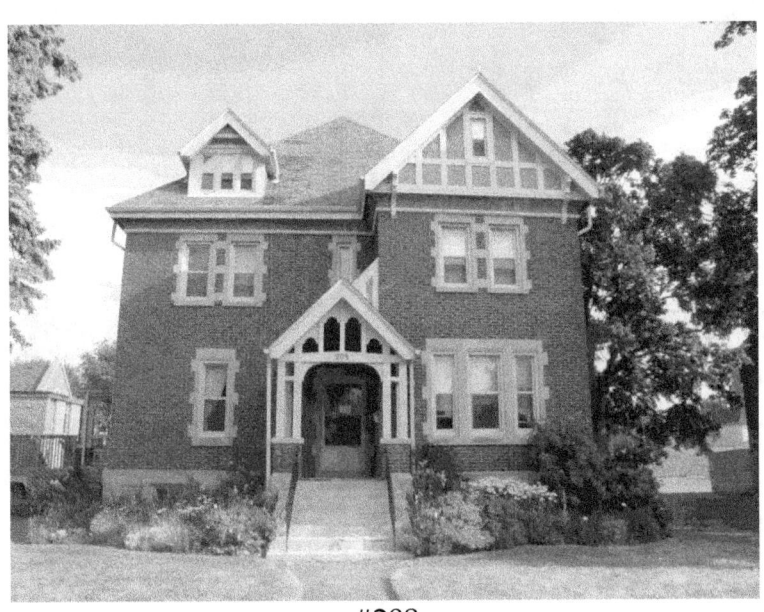

#208

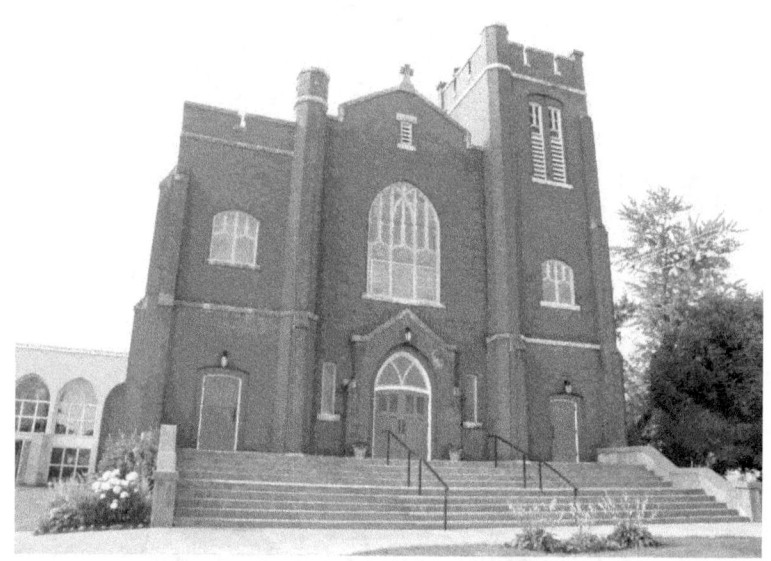

St. James United Church

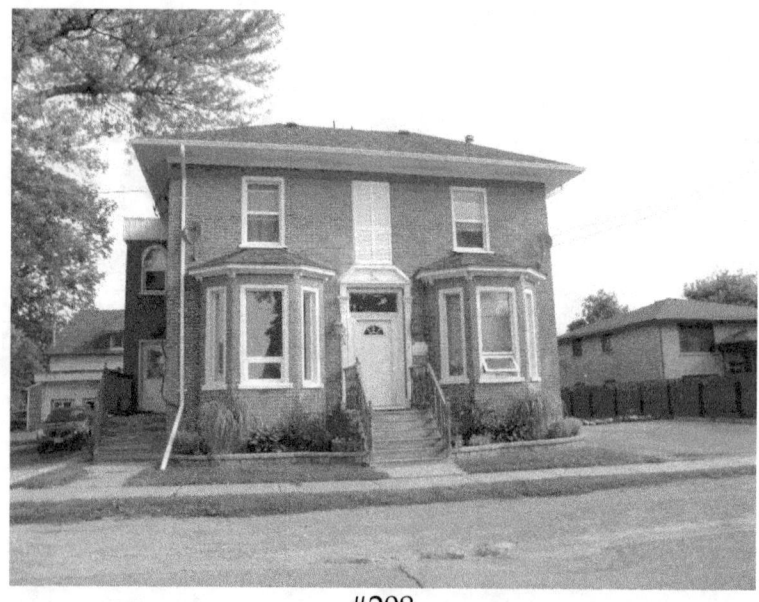

#208

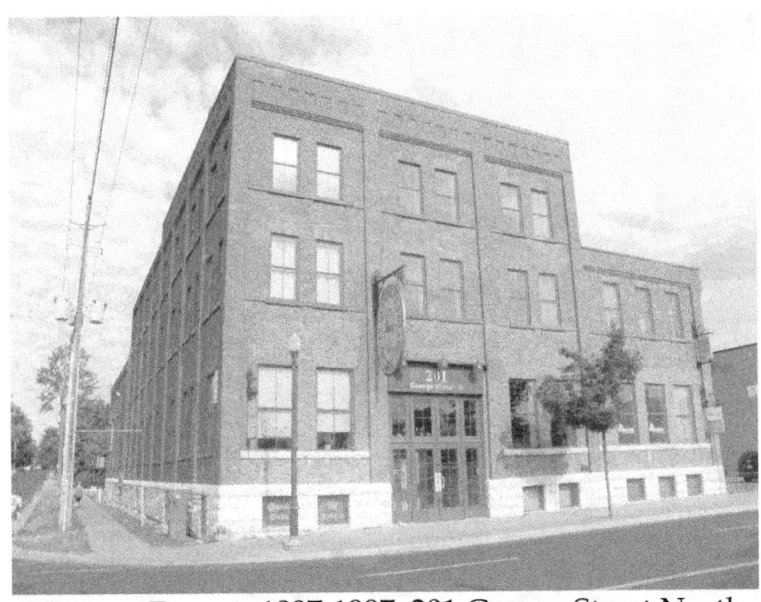

Harness Factory 1897-1997, 201 George Street North

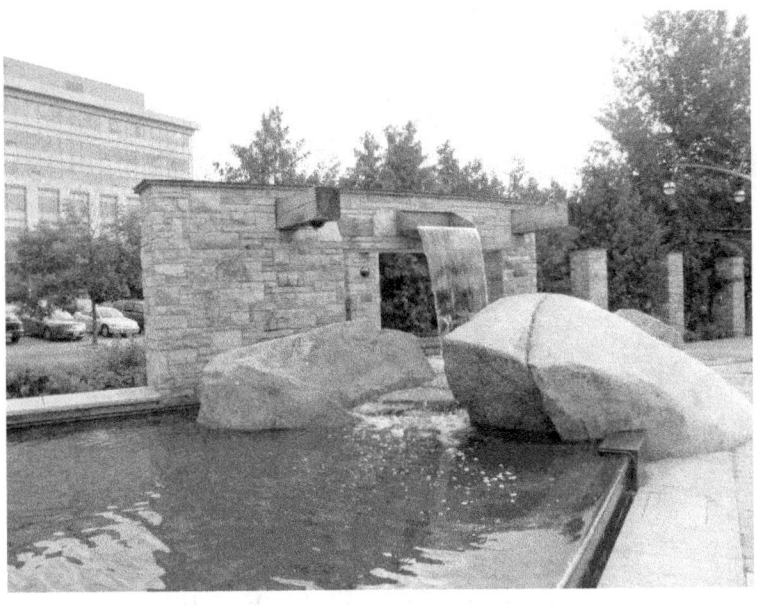

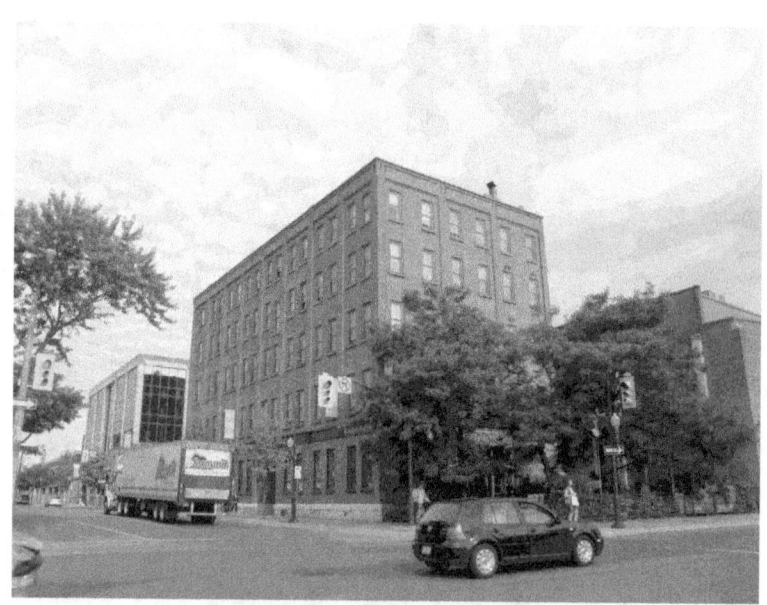
Corner of Water Street

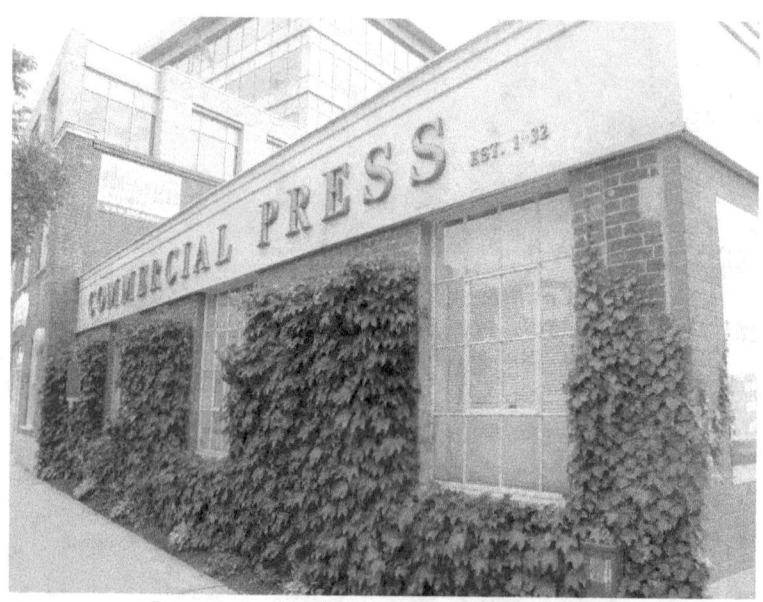
Commercial Press established 1932

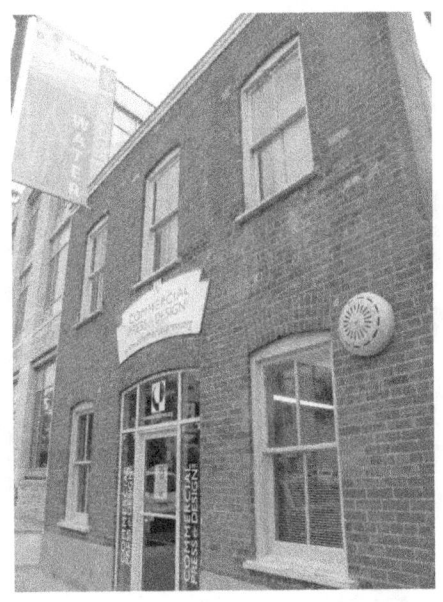

Near this site in 1820, the community's first resident, Adam Scott built a saw mill and a gristmill. The small settlement that grew around them was known as Scott's Plains until 1826 when it was renamed in honour of Peter Robinson. Although of primitive construction, the mills were of great benefit to the early settlers including the Irish immigrants brought over by Robinson in 1825. Scott relinquished possession of the mills in 1827 and in 1835 they were destroyed by fire.

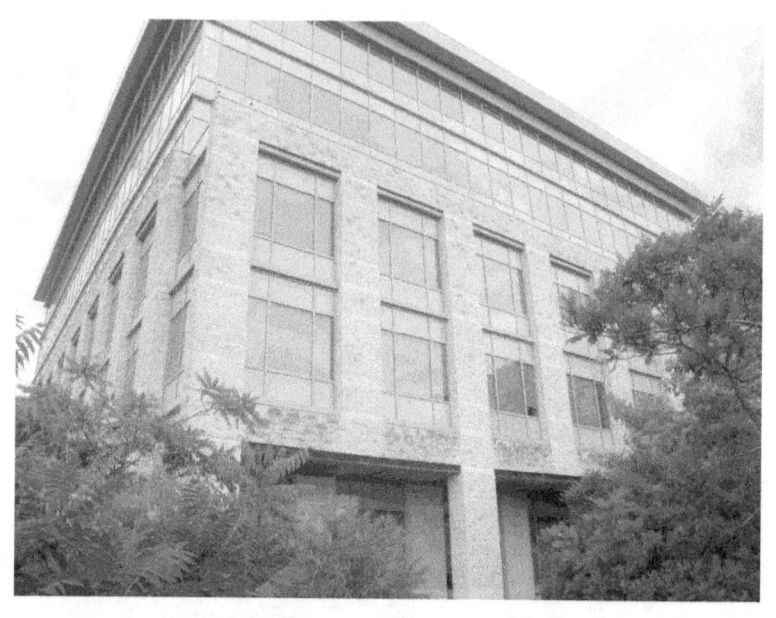

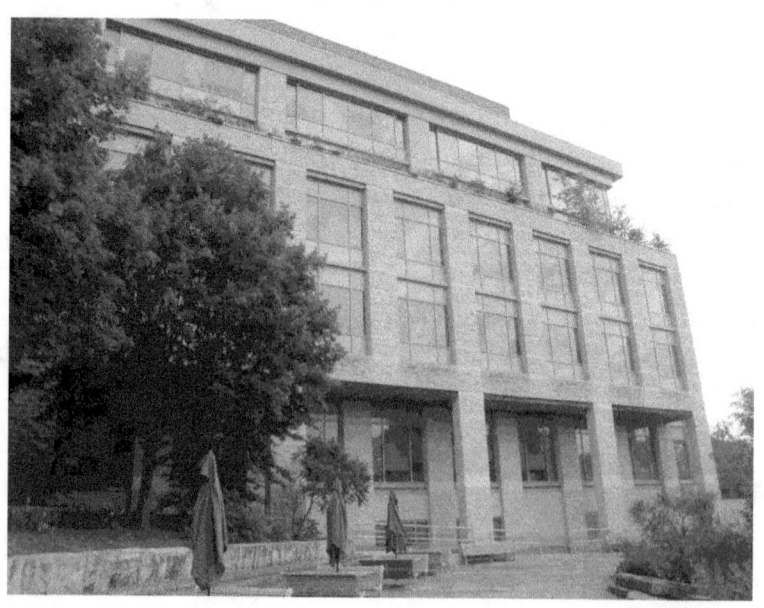

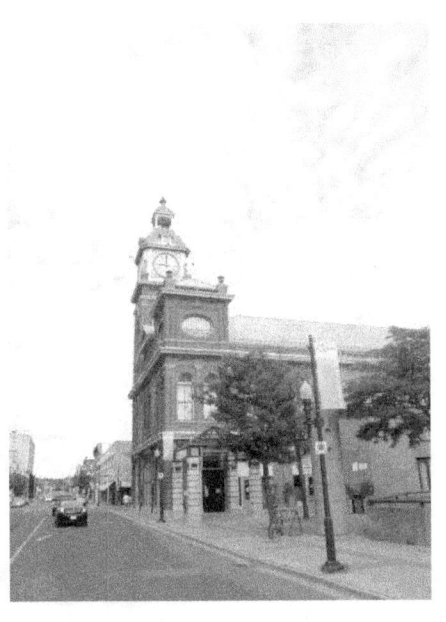

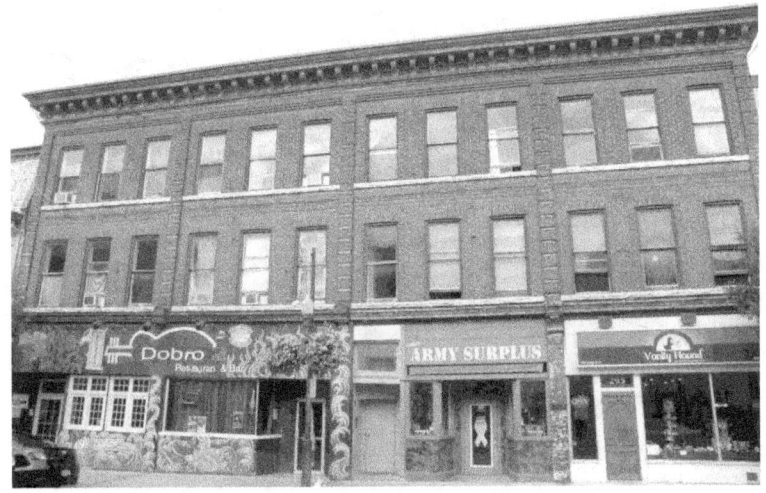

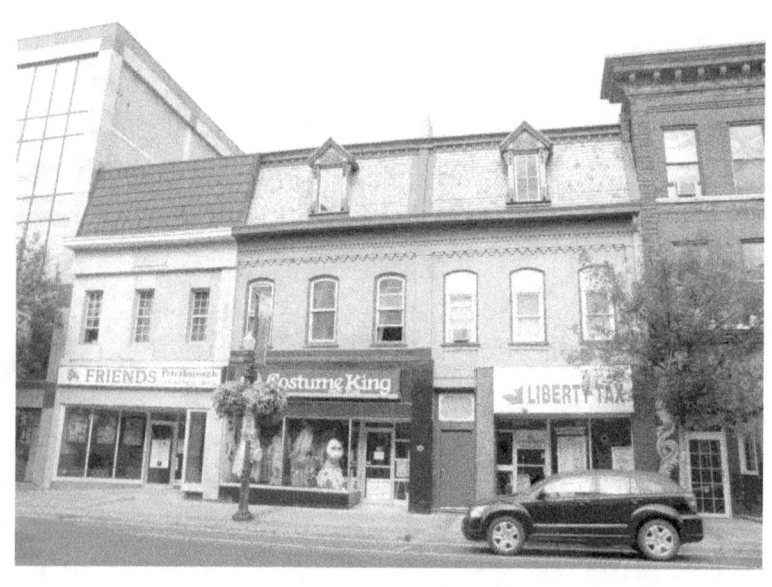

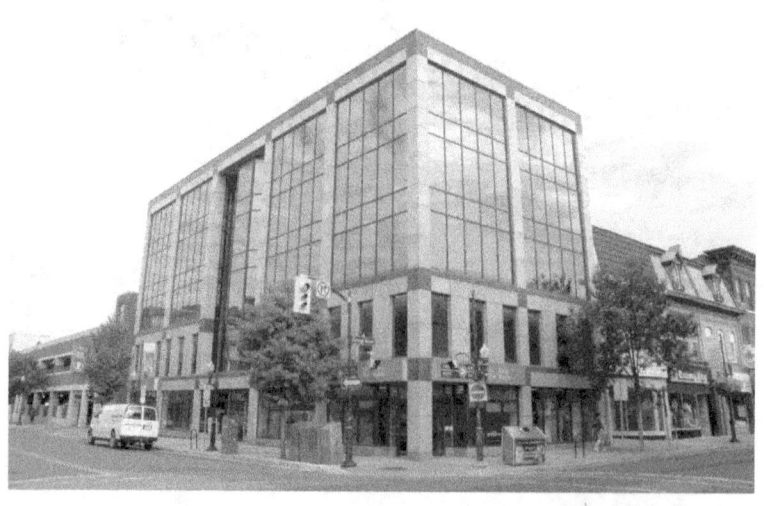

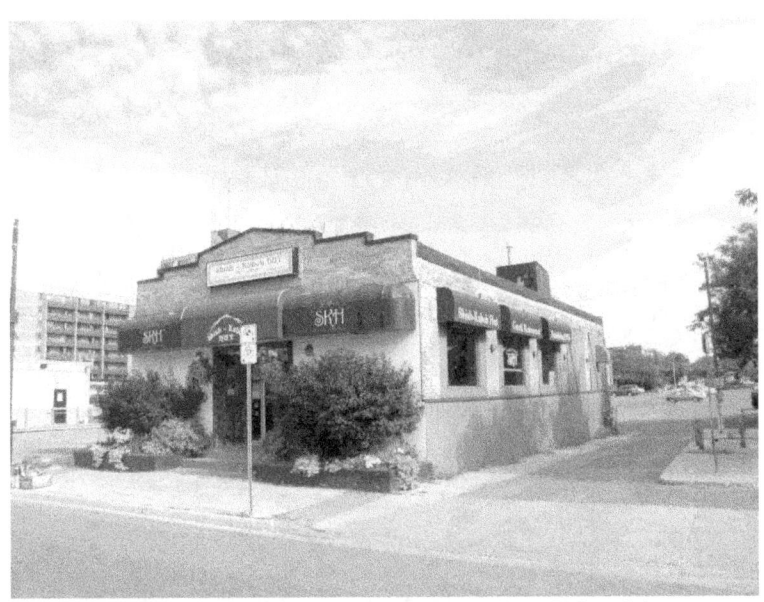

Shish-Kabob Hut – old yellow brick building

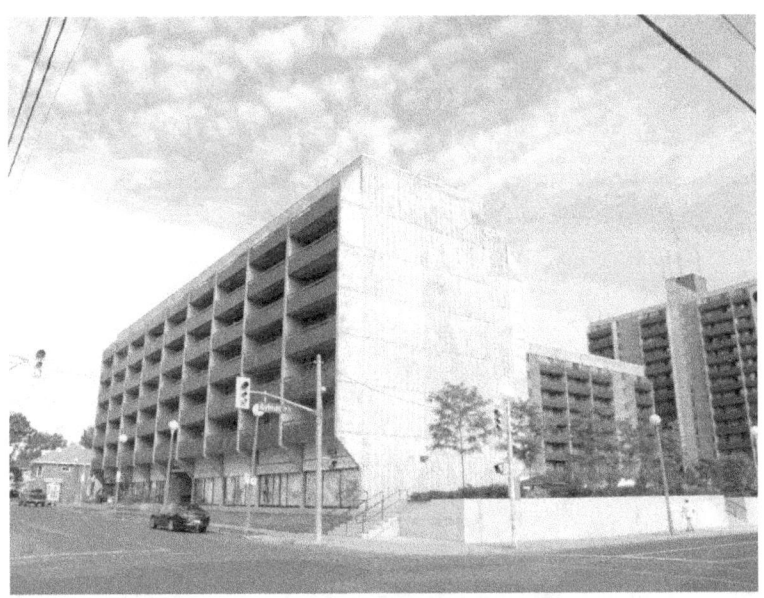

Corner of Aylmer Street

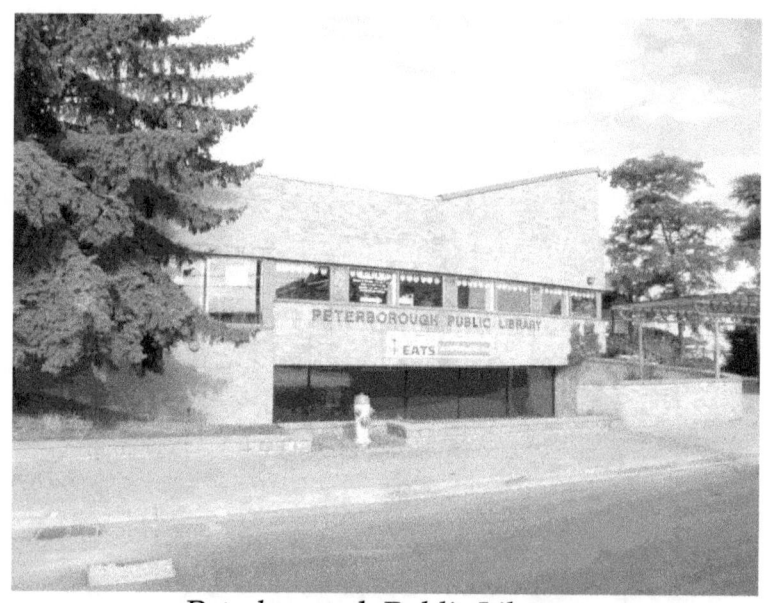

Peterborough Public Library
345 Aylmer Street North opened on September 2, 1980

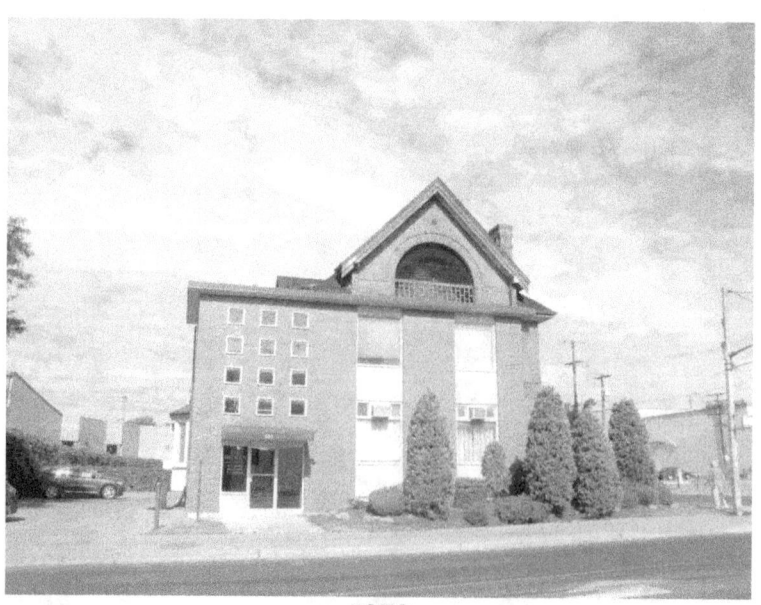

#359

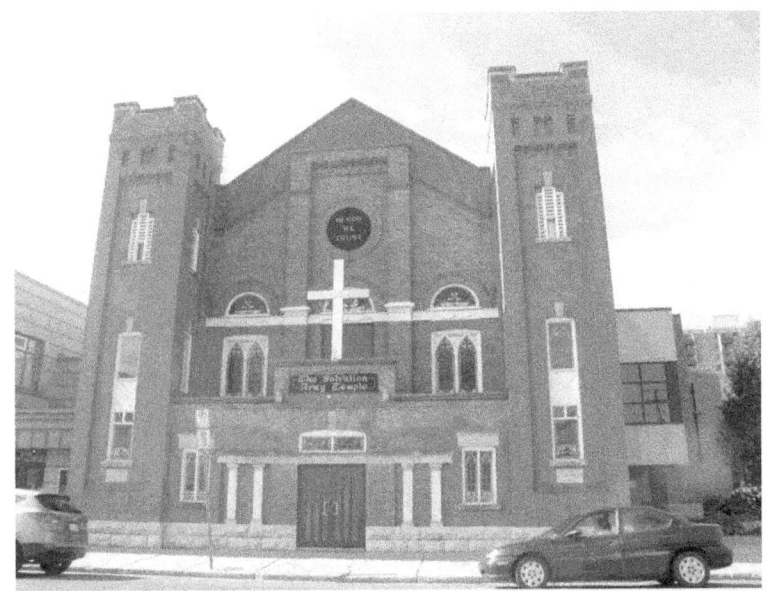

The Salvation Army Peterborough Temple erected 1888

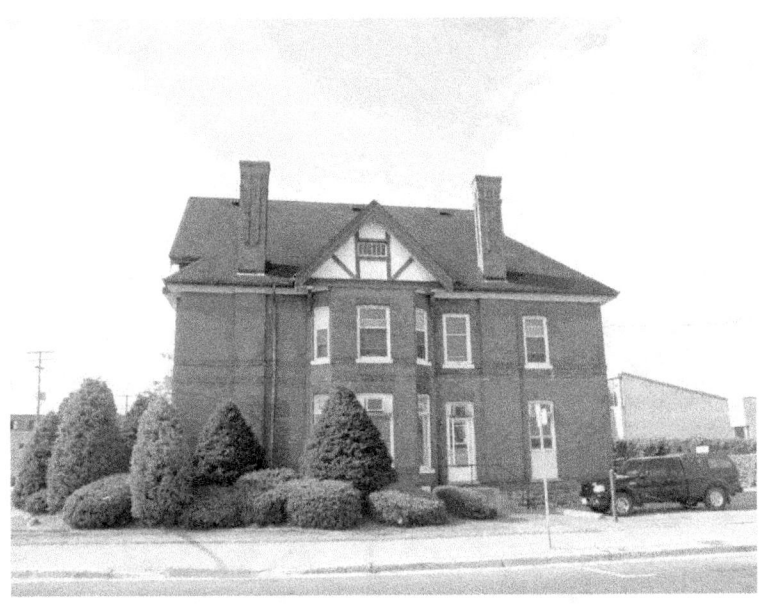

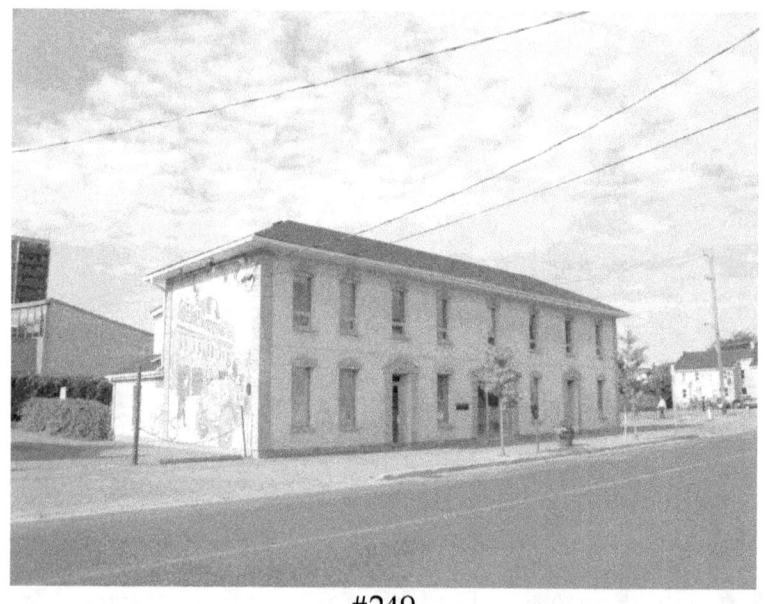

#249
Mural of an old fire truck and building on the end wall

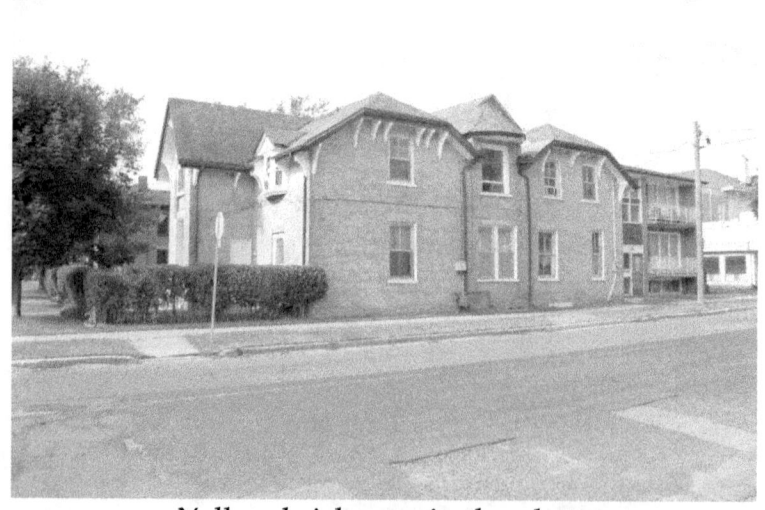

Yellow brick, cornice brackets

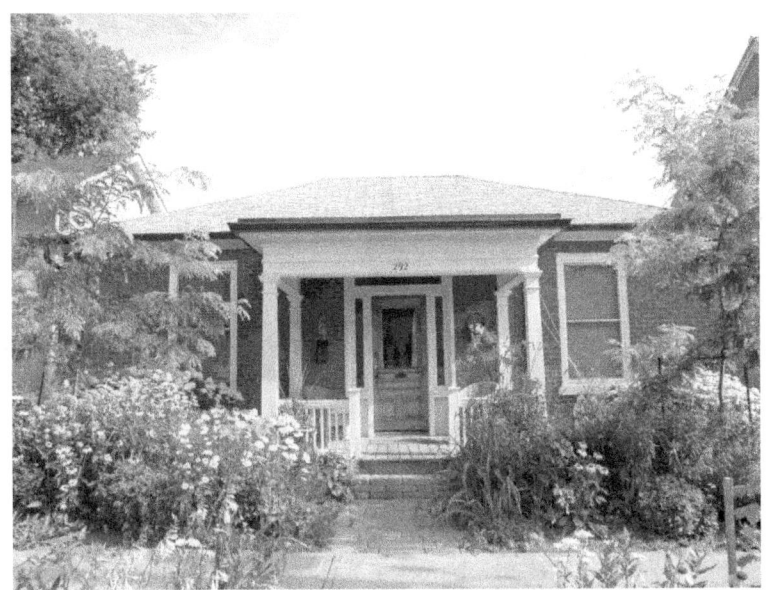

#292 – lots of flowers to add beauty

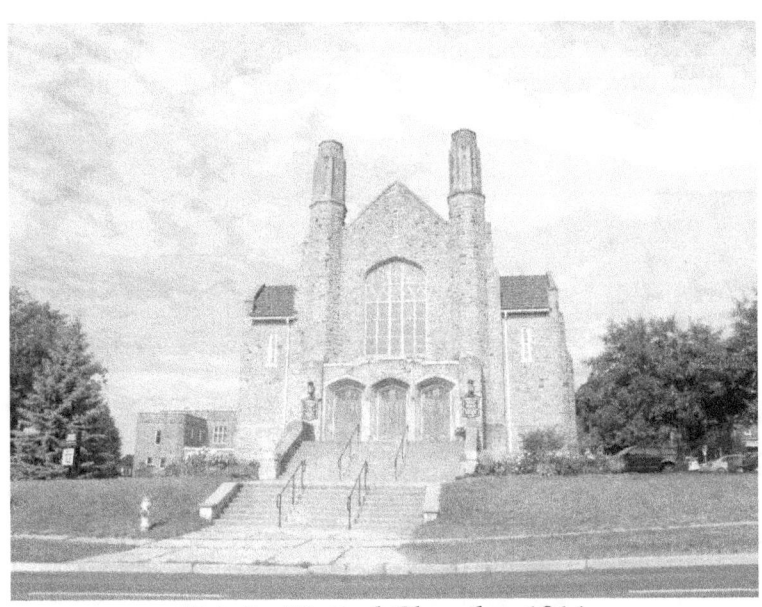

Trinity United Church – 1914

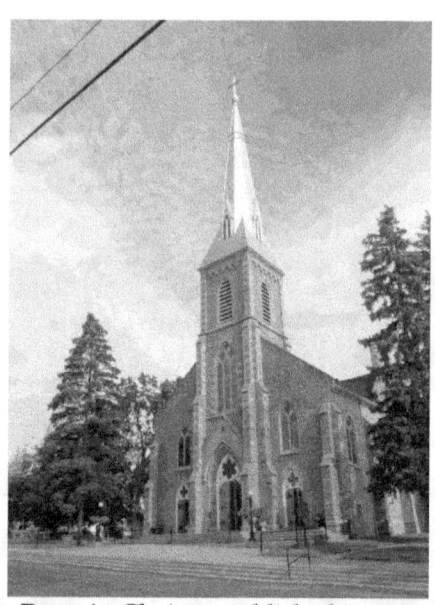

The Cathedral of St. Peter-in-Chains established in 1826 to serve the large Irish Catholic population of the surrounding Robinson settlement. This building erected in 1837-38 of stone from nearby Jackson's Creek is one of the oldest remaining Catholic churches in Ontario. It follows the modified Gothic Revival style popular in Upper Canada during the period. In 1882 when the Diocese of Peterborough was created, St. Peter's became a cathedral. Although altered on various occasions, St. Peter's-in-Chains has retained its original elegance and imposing form.

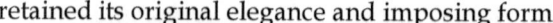

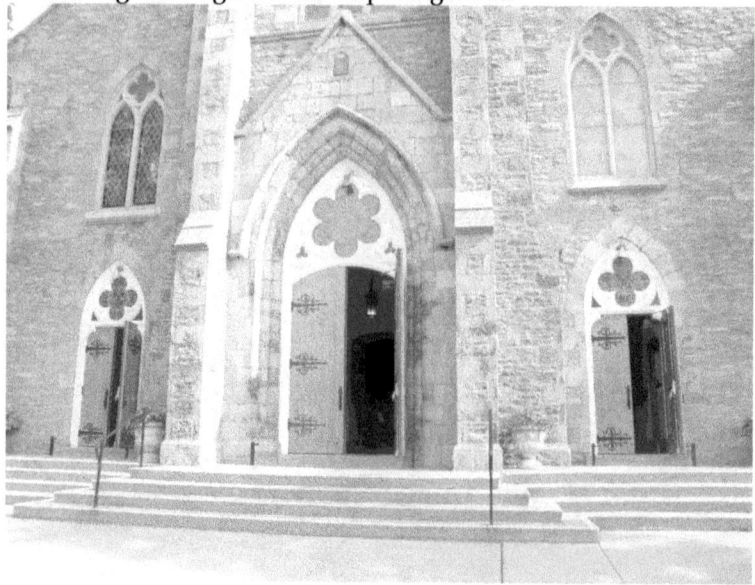

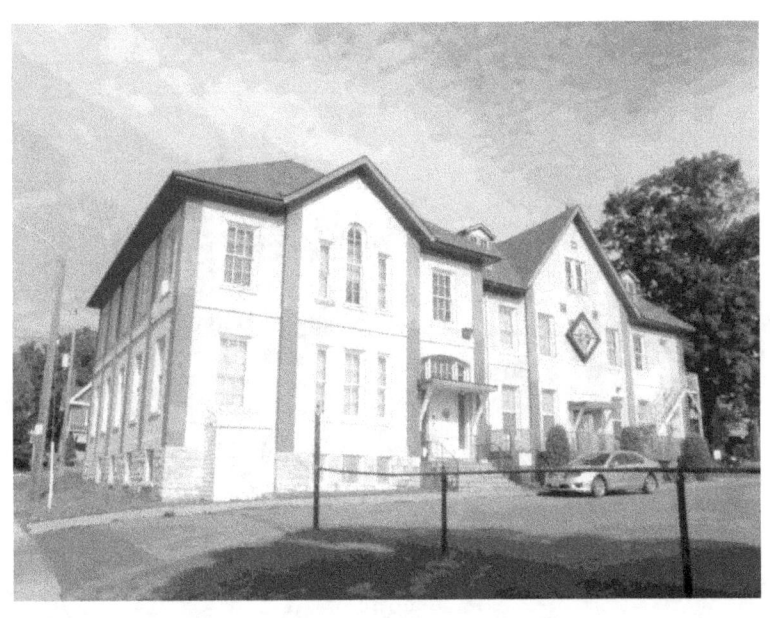

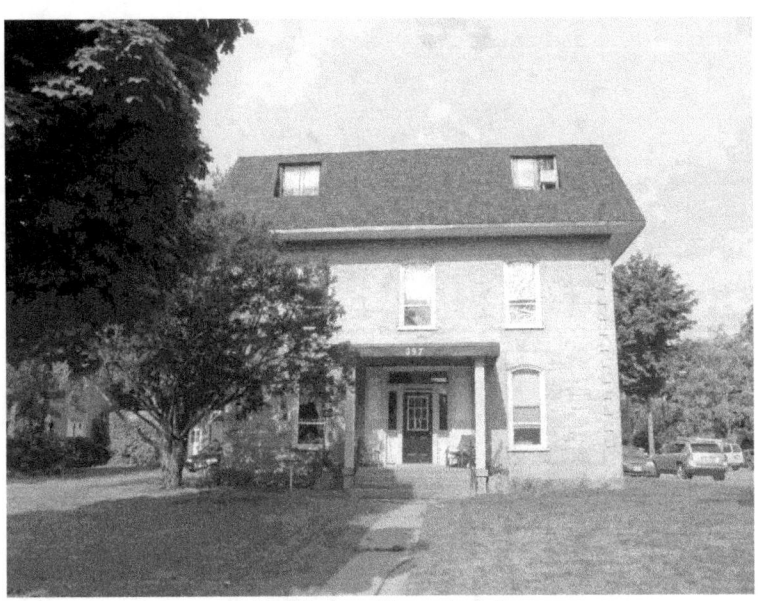

#397 – yellow brick

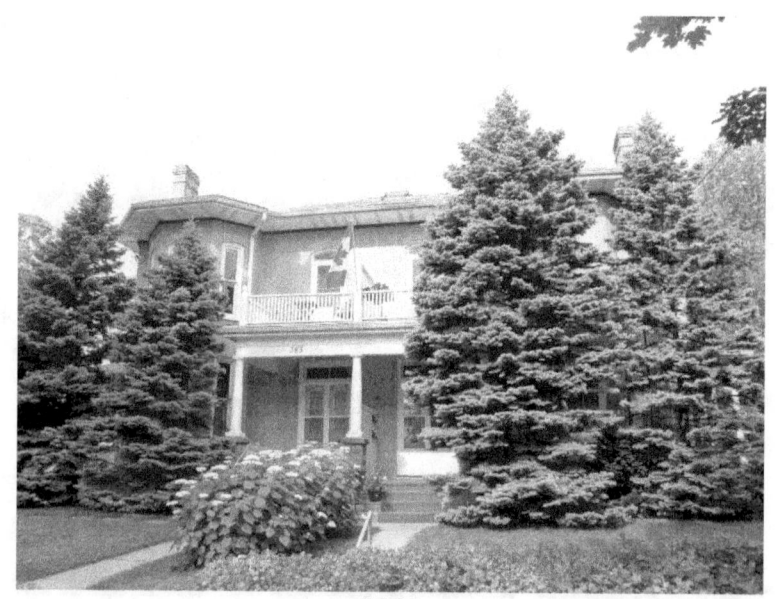

#385

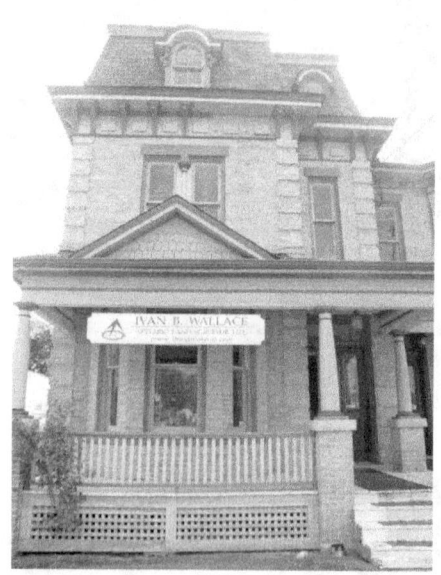

#338

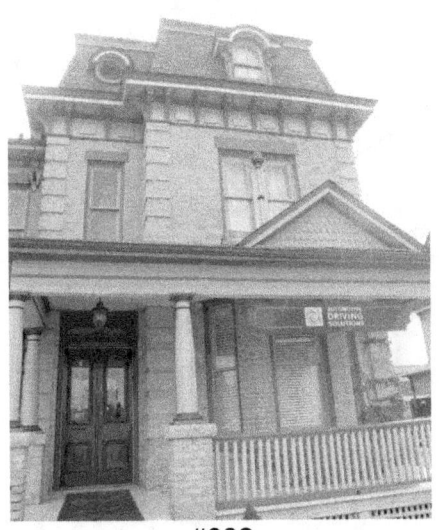

#332

An elegant example of a residential terrace in the Second
Empire style, Cox Terrace, 332-344 Rubidge Street, was
constructed in 1884 during a time of prosperity and rapid
urban growth in Peterborough. In this row of houses,
inspired by British models, seven dwellings are skillfully
unified behind one façade with three projecting pavilions.
Mansard roofs, dormers, and oriel windows give life to the
distinctive design. The terrace was built for Sir George Cox,
one of the wealthiest and most influential Canadian
businessmen of the period.

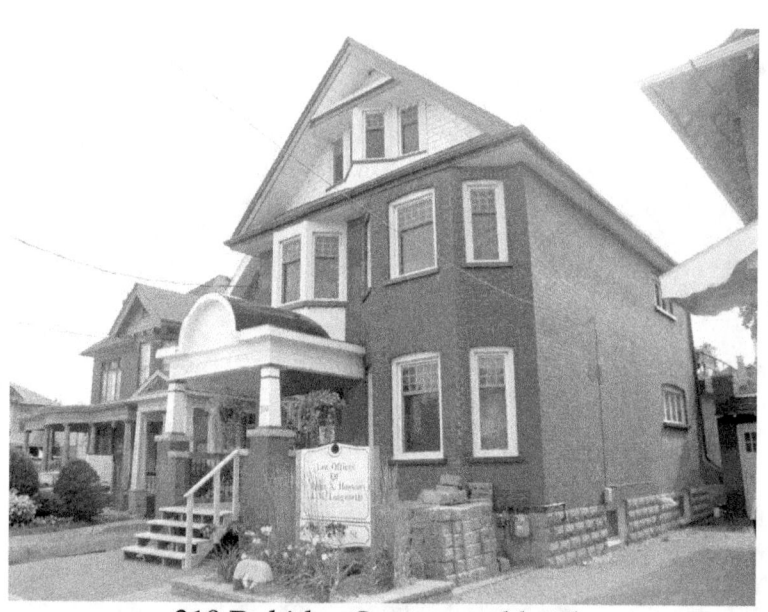

310 Rubidge Street – red brick

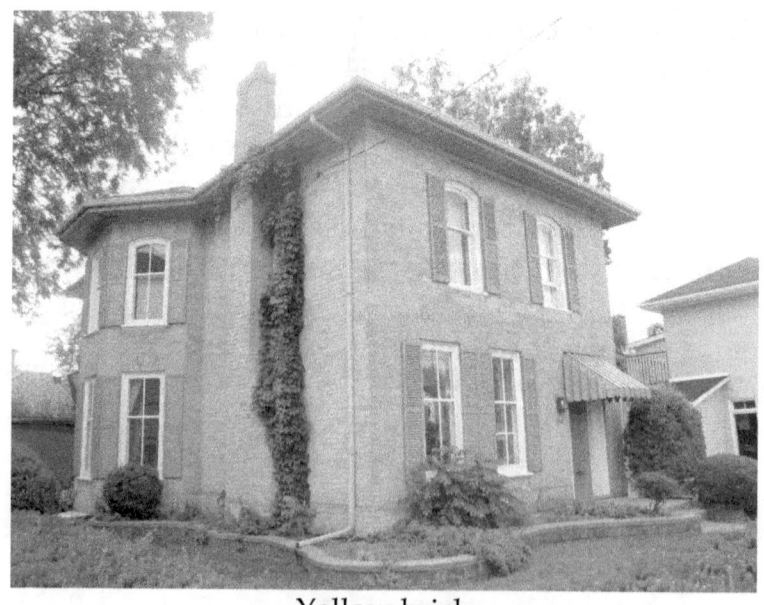

Yellow brick

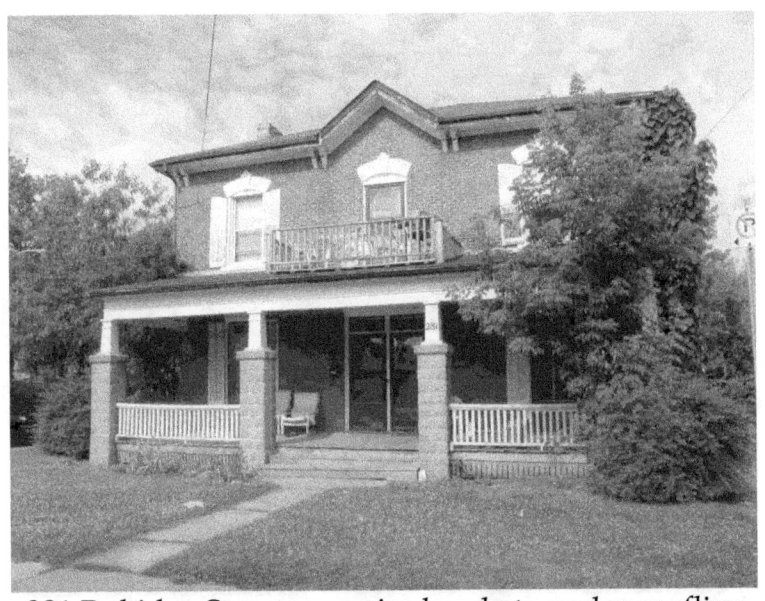

281 Rubidge Street – cornice brackets under roofline

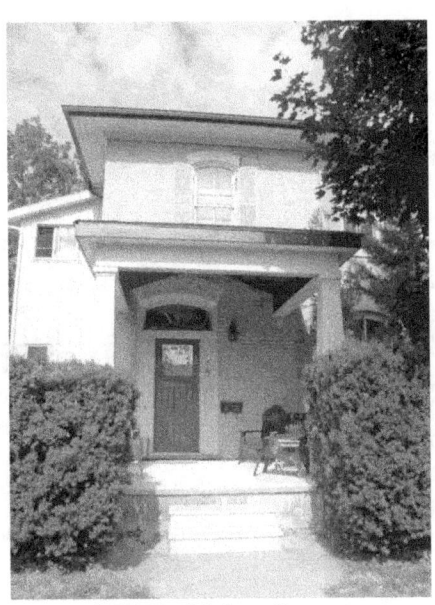

277 Rubidge Street

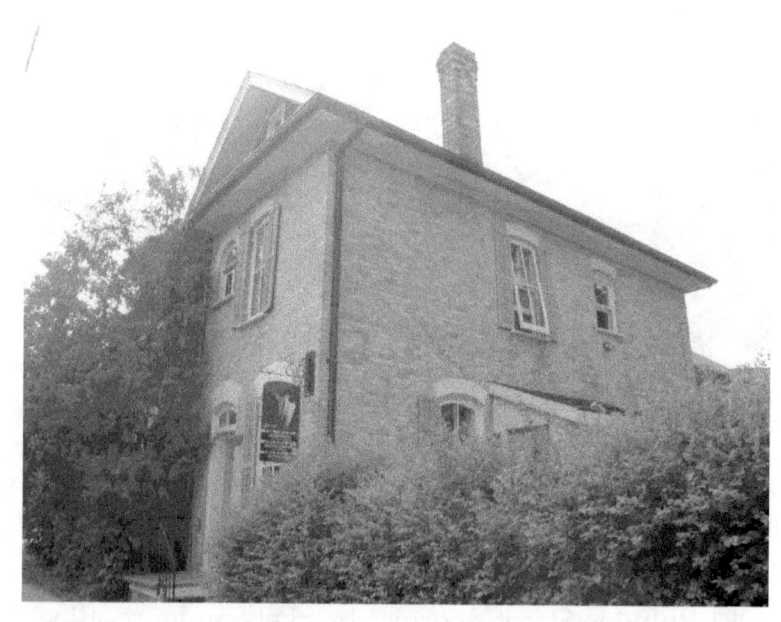

315 Rubidge Street - yellow brick

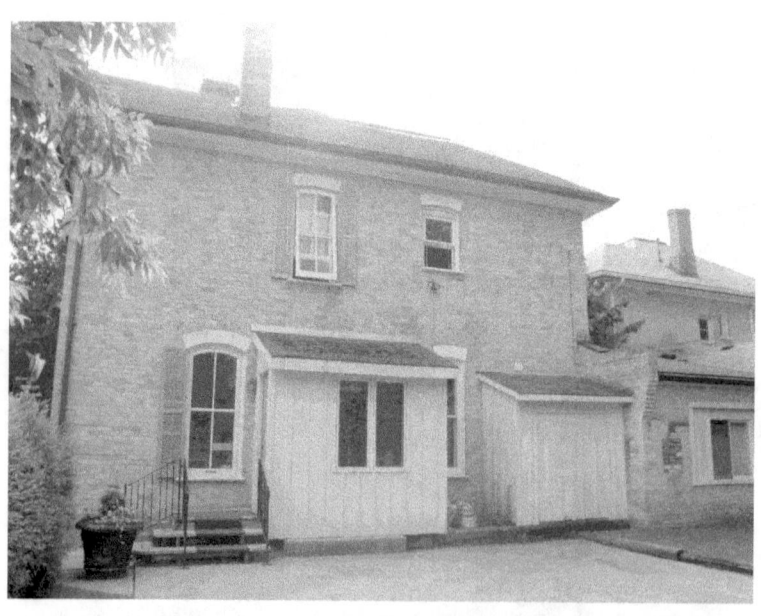

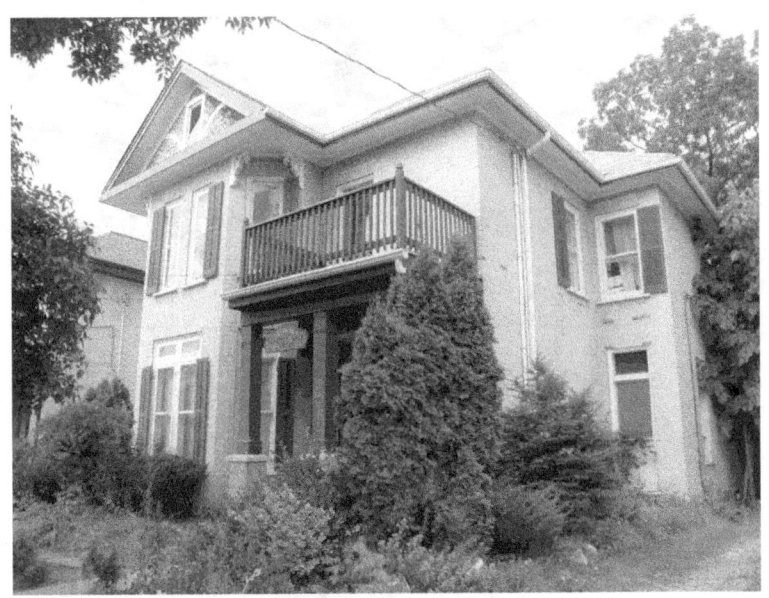

273 Rubidge Street

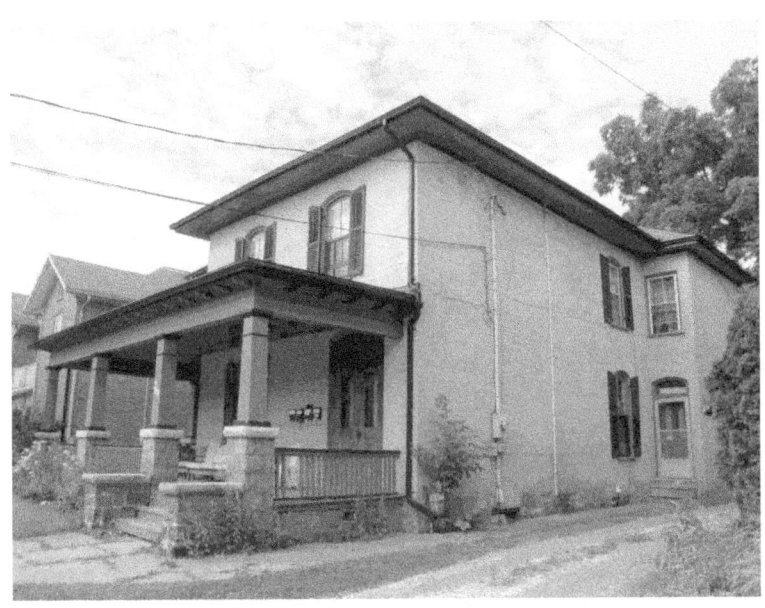

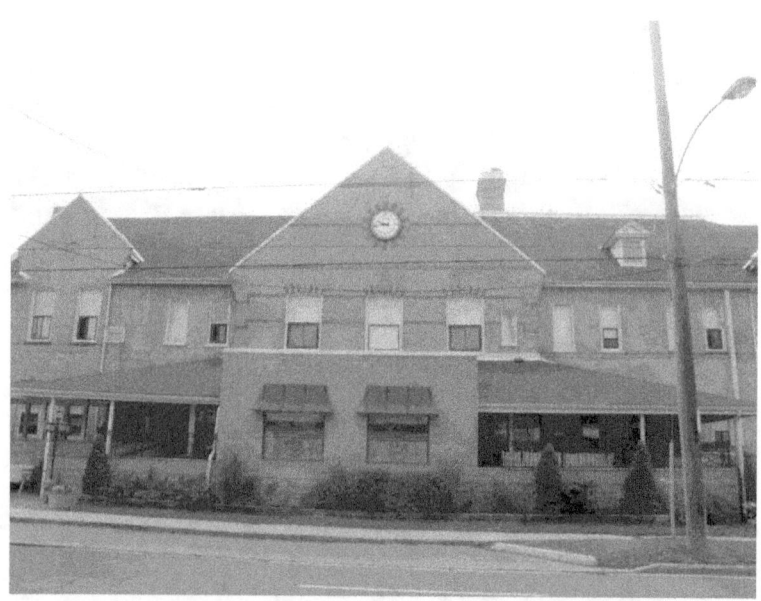

Dichromatic brick work – two colours of brick

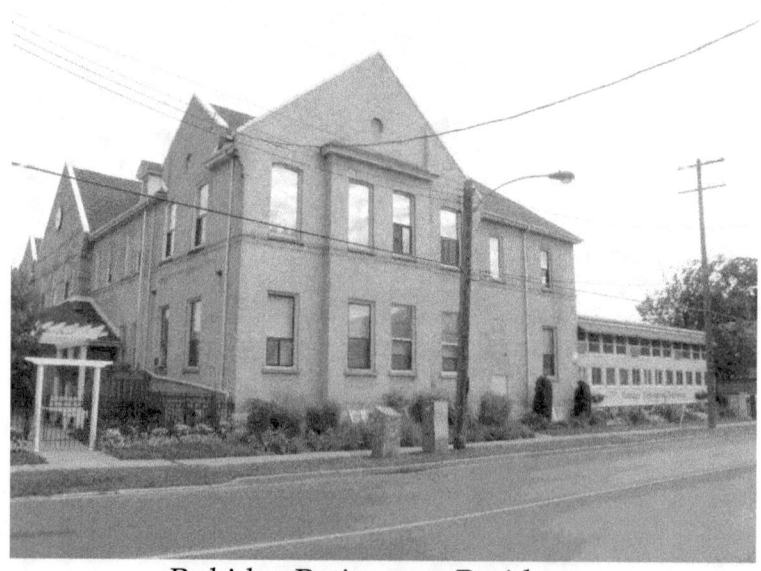

Rubidge Retirement Residence

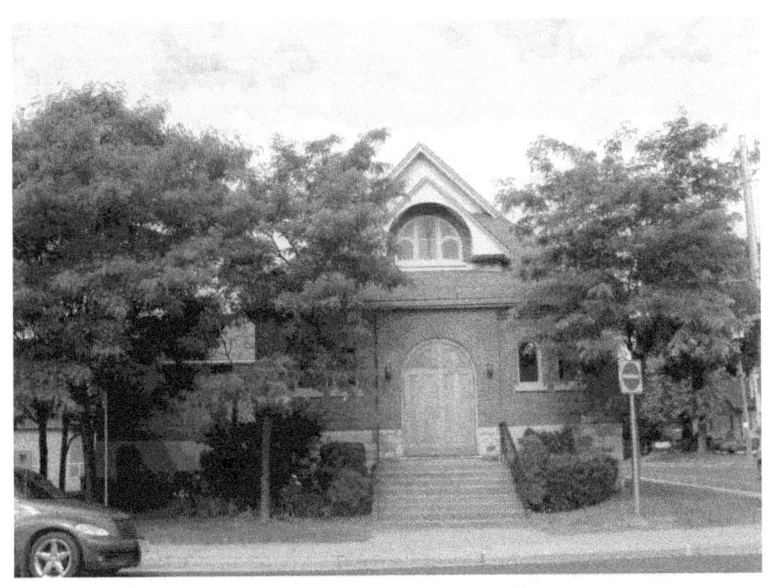

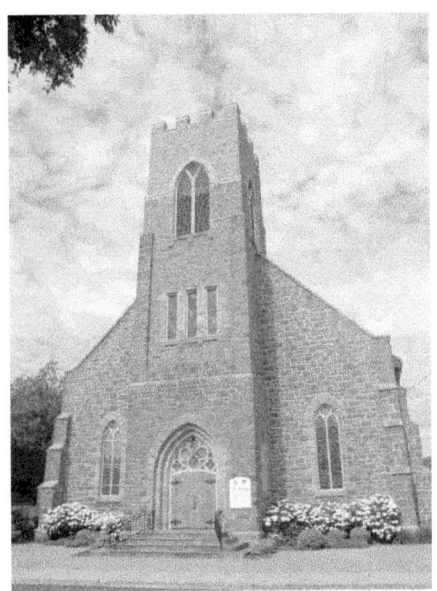

All Saints Church, 235 Rubidge Street

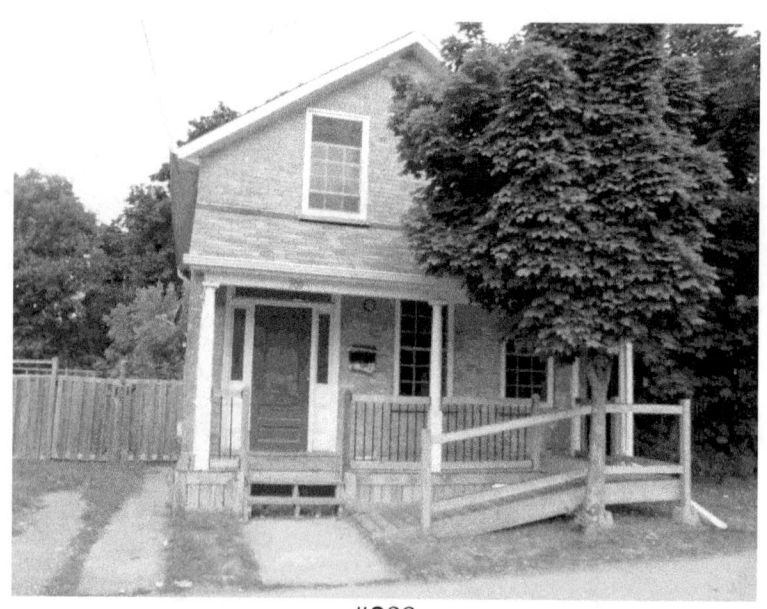

#209

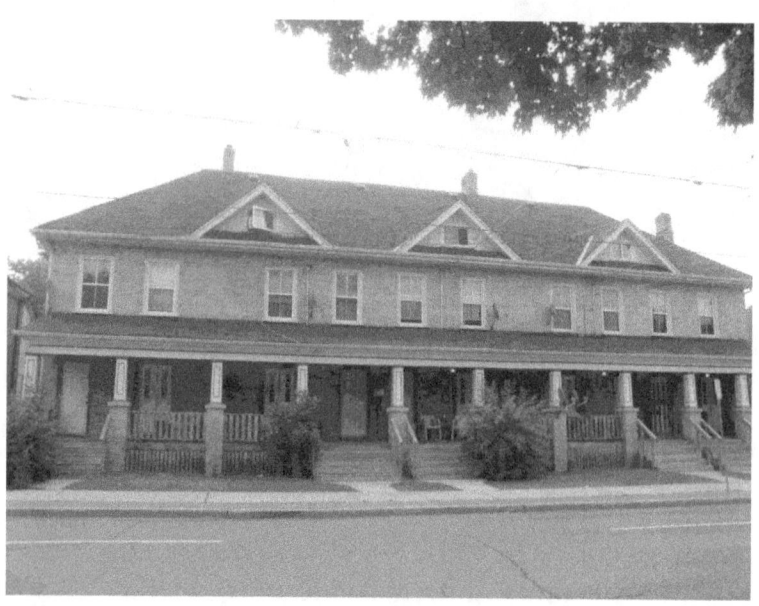

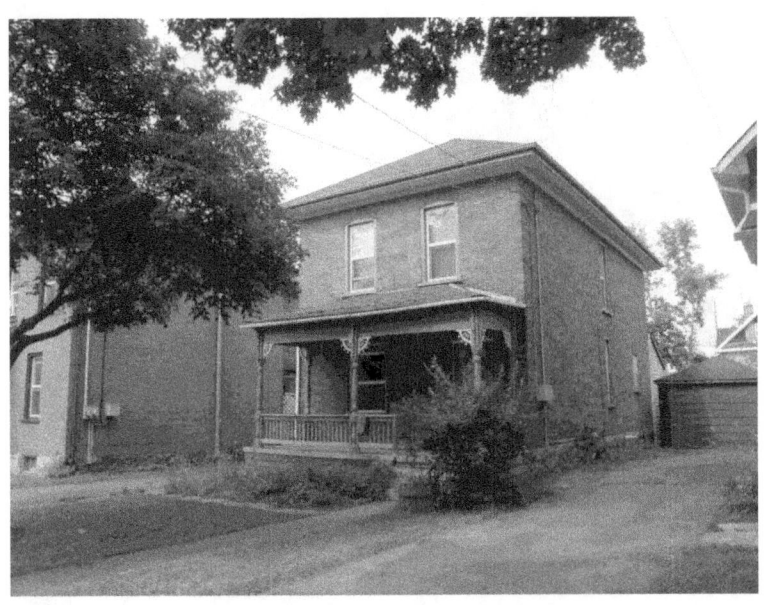

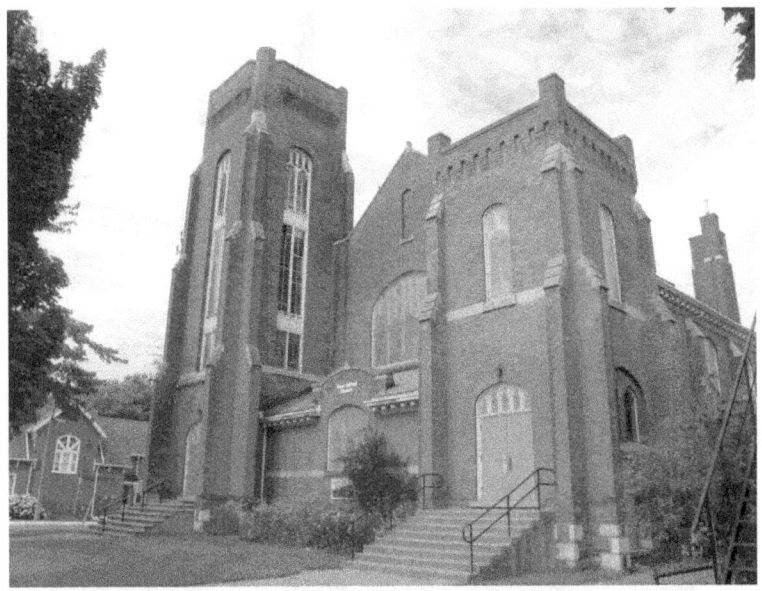

Knox United Church – 1910 – 400 Wolfe Street

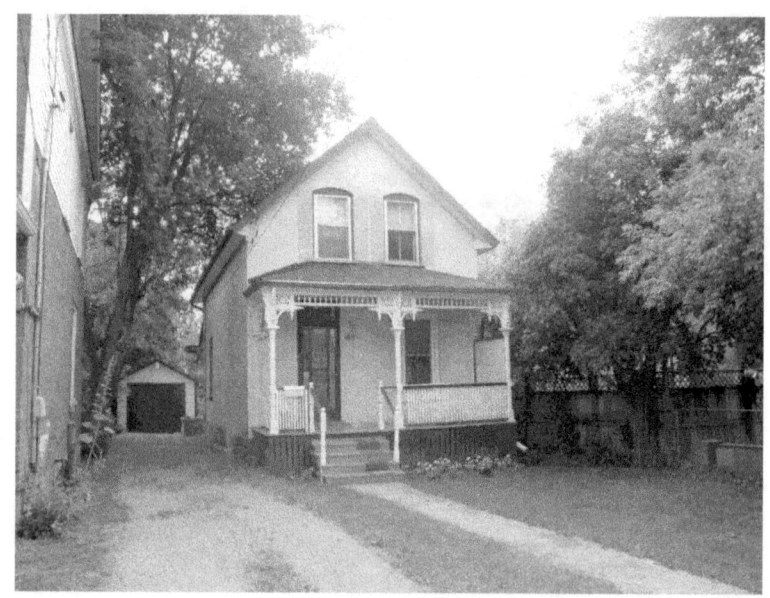

#168

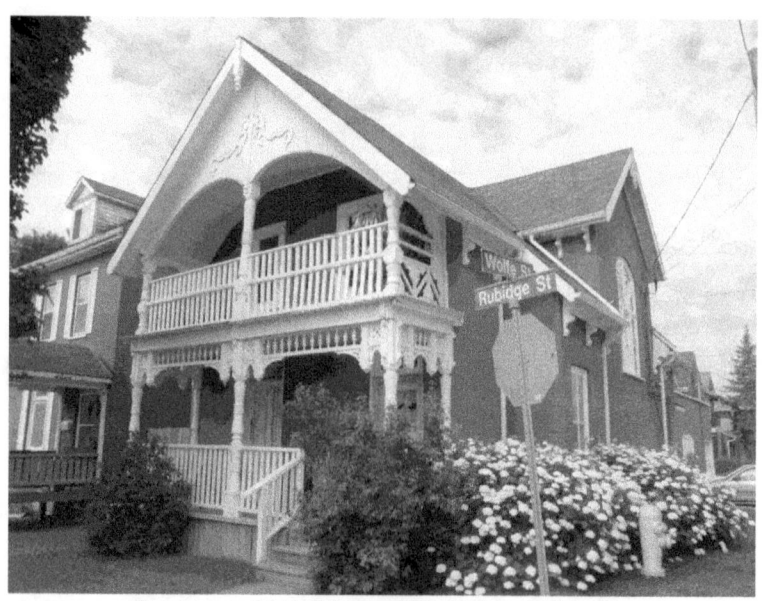

Corner of Wolfe and Rubidge Streets

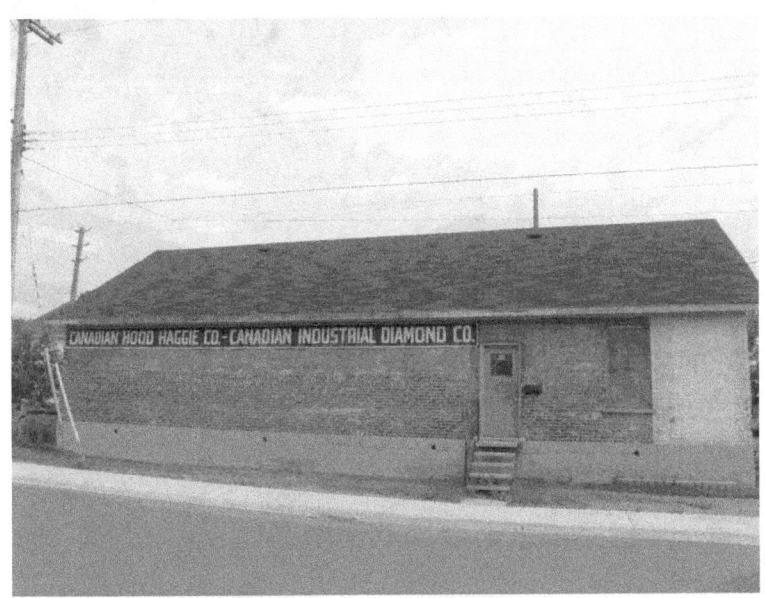

Canadian Hood Haggie Co. – Canadian Industrial Diamond
Co. – 250 Wolfe Street – old brown brick

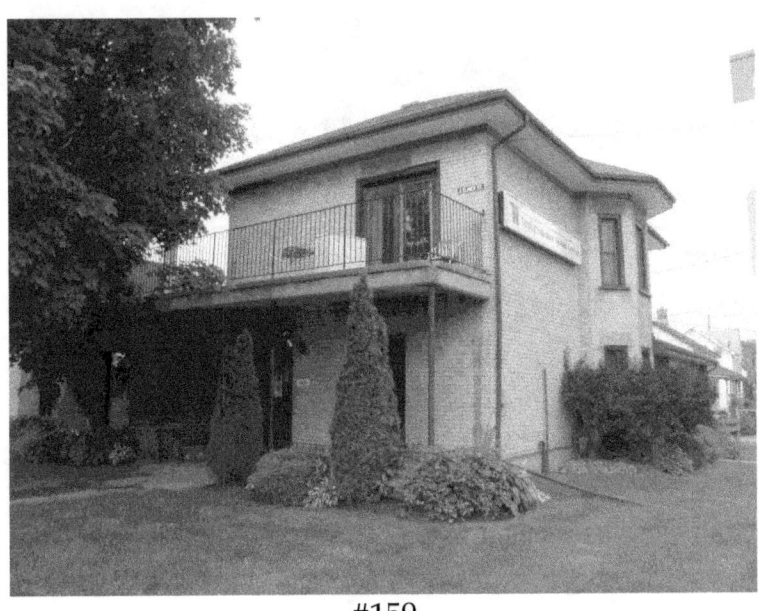

#159

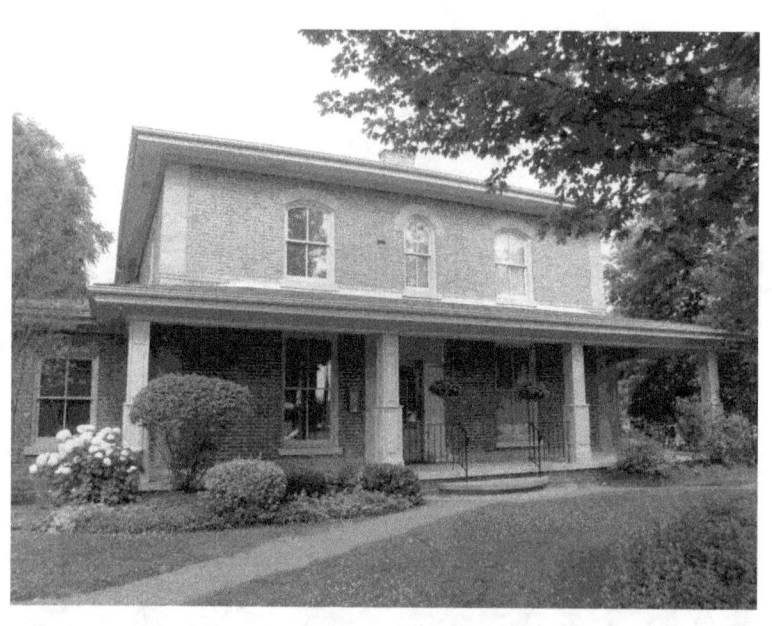

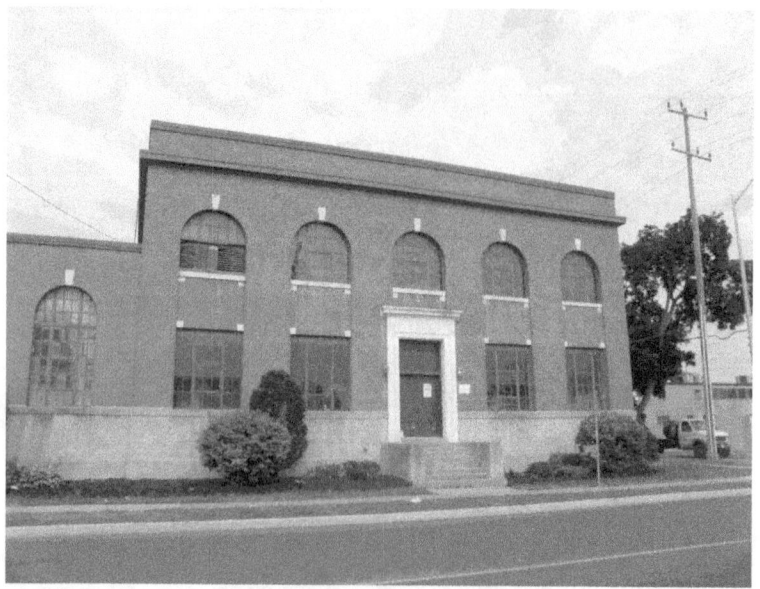

Peterborough Utilities Commission – A.D. 1923

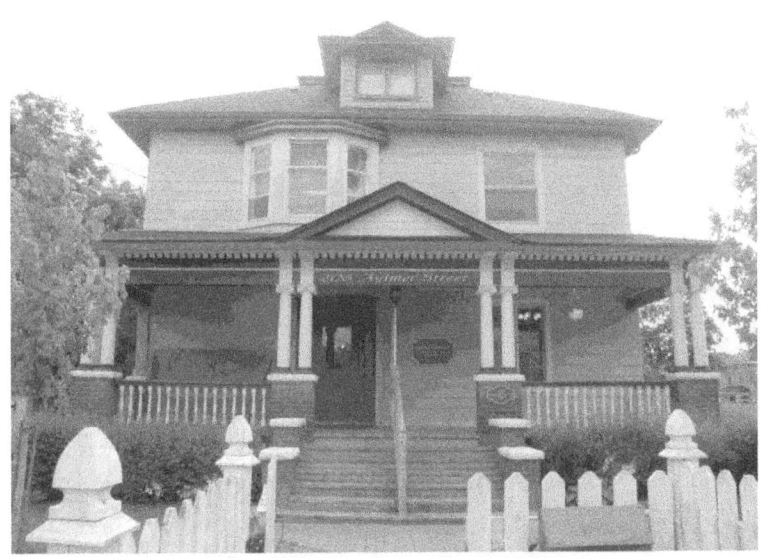

The Madge House – 1837
206 Aylmer Street

Robert P. Madge was a retired English lieutenant of the Royal Navy who originally settled on Sandy Lake in Harvey Township in about 1832. The Madge House is one of the oldest houses in the City of Peterborough. Huge hand hewn timbers were used in the construction of the house, a very large frame house of the 1830s. The Madge House appeared on the assessment rolls in 1838 as a two-storey frame house with one additional fireplace. Robert P. Madge was listed as both the owner and occupant.

The Madge House was originally covered with rough cast plaster. The side windows were French doors opening onto upper and lower verandas which encircled the house on three sides.

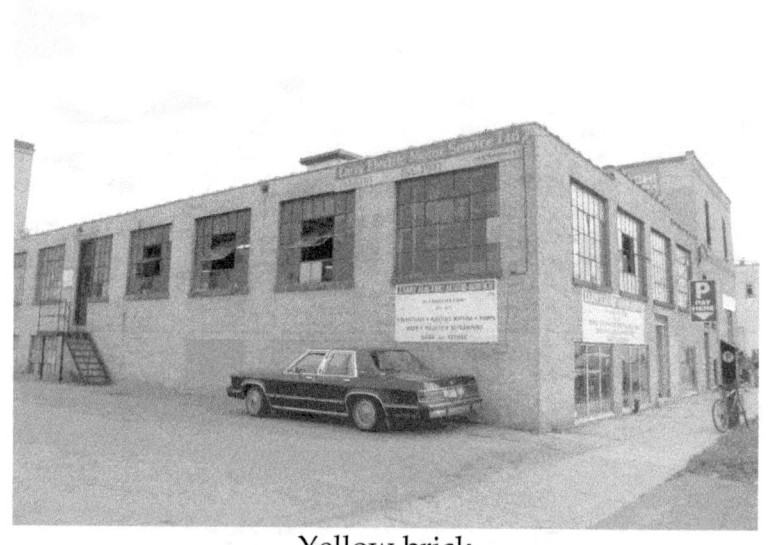

Yellow brick

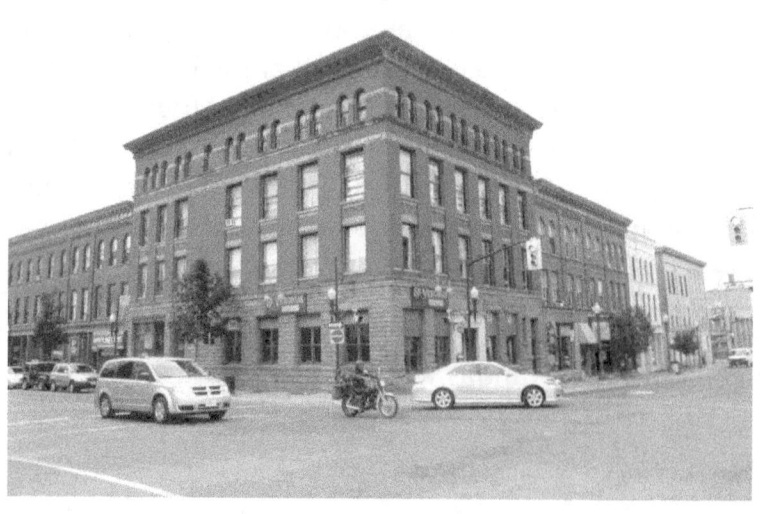

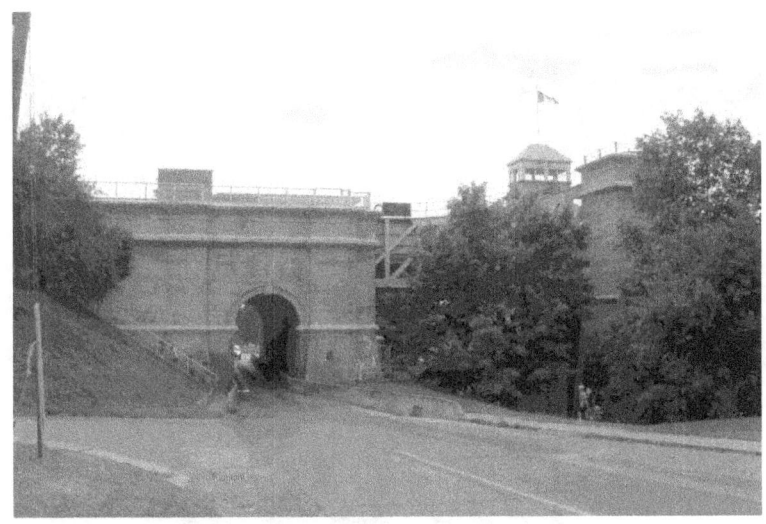

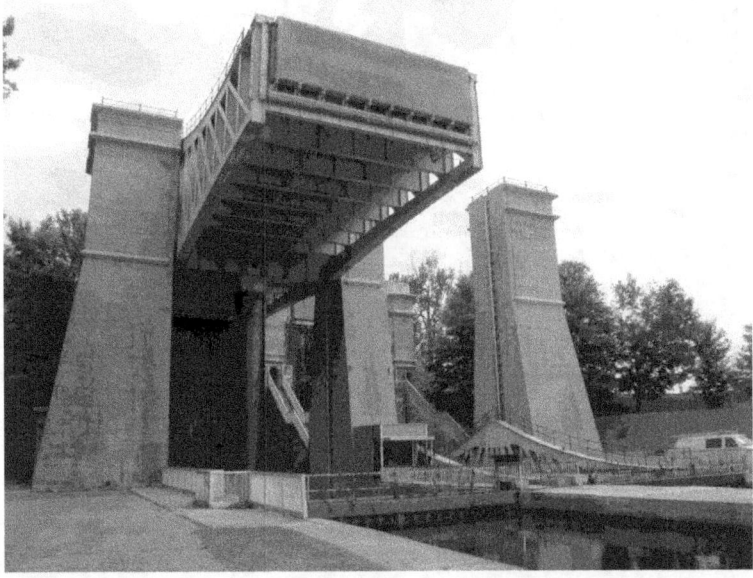

The Peterborough Lift Lock was completed on July 9, 1904. It was the first lock to be built out of concrete and at the time was the largest structure built in the world with unreinforced concrete. It is a boat lift located on the Trent Canal in the city of Peterborough and is Lock 21 on the Trent-Severn Waterway. The dual lifts are the highest hydraulic boat lifts in the world, with a lift of 19.8 m (65 ft).

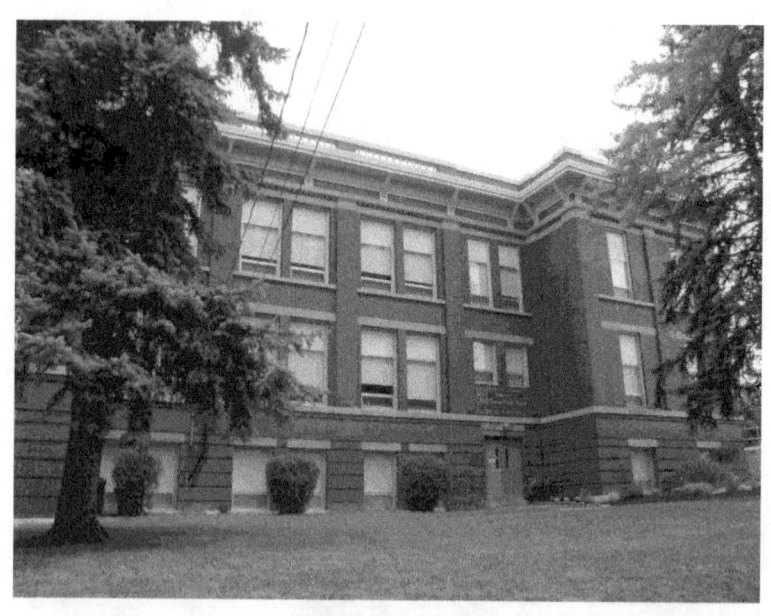

King George Public School

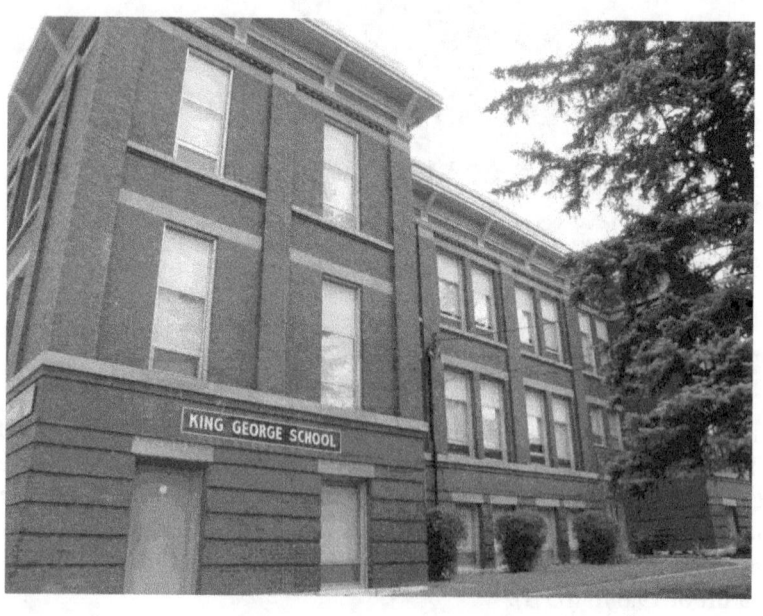

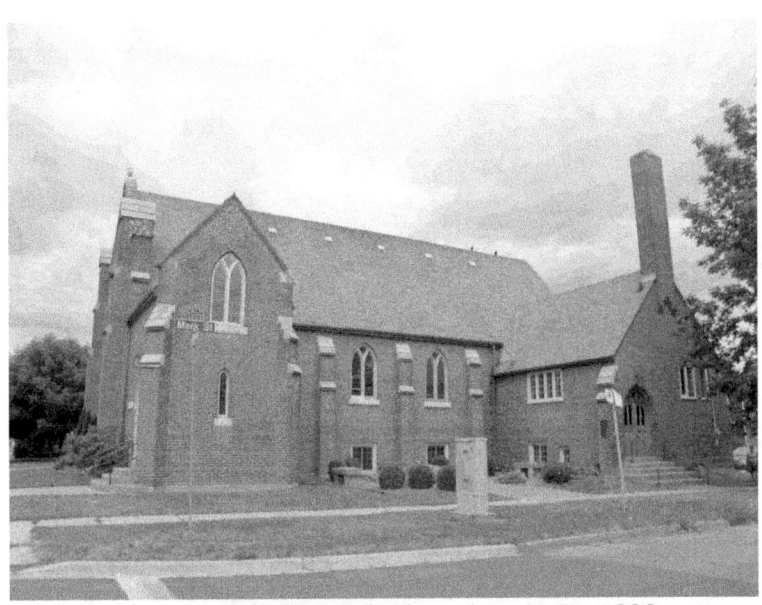

Mark Street United Church – A. D. 1928

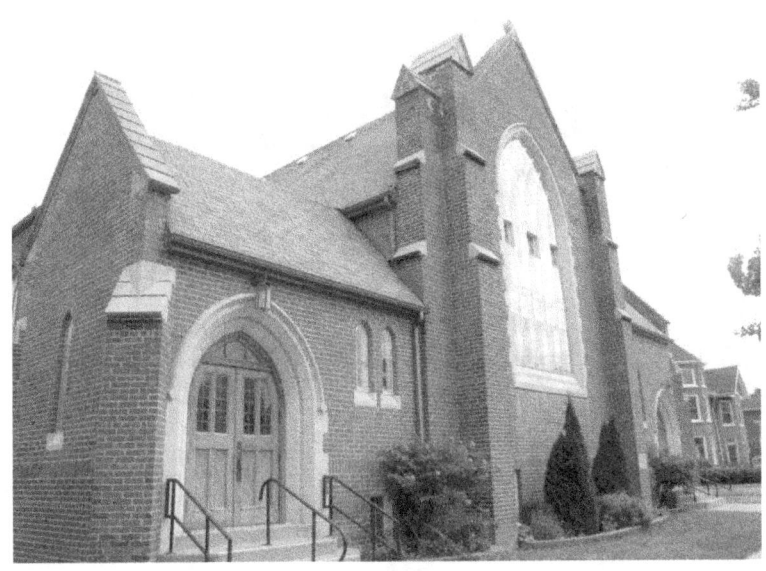

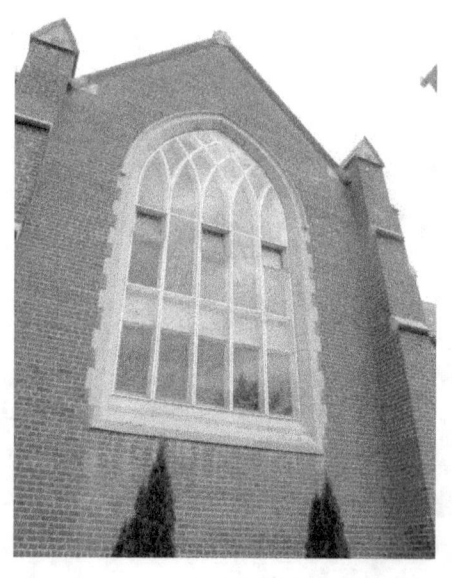

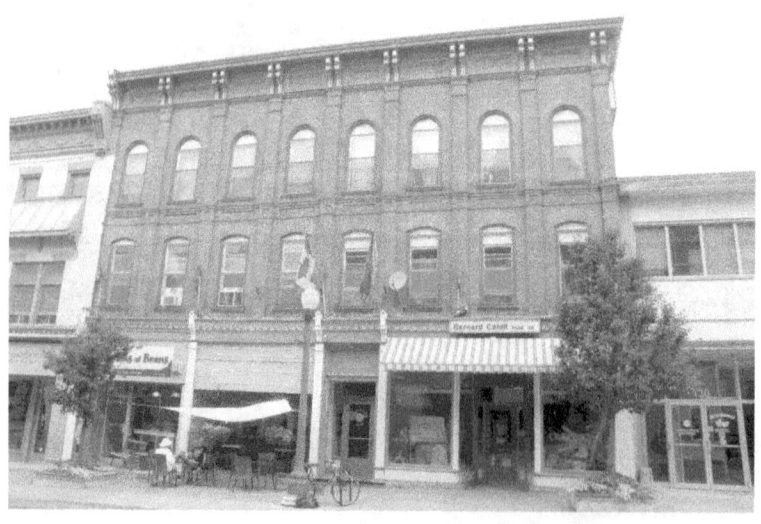

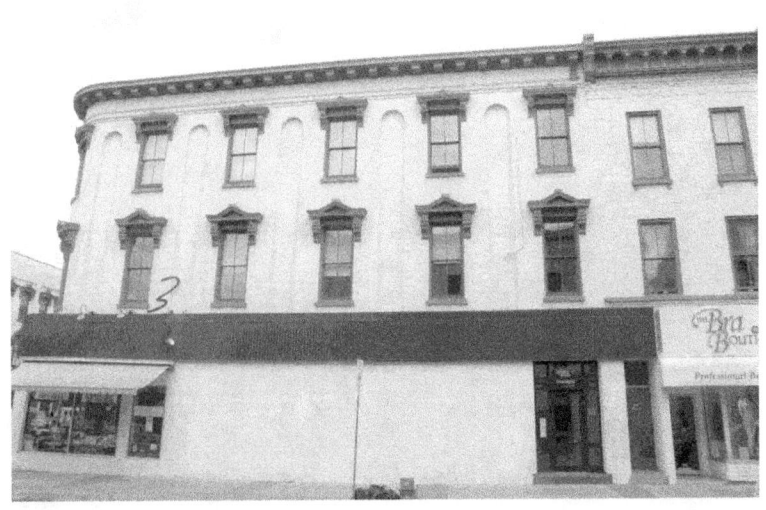

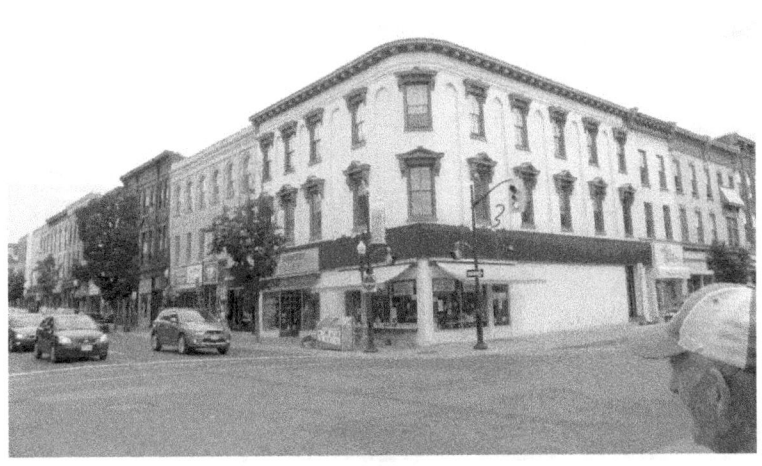

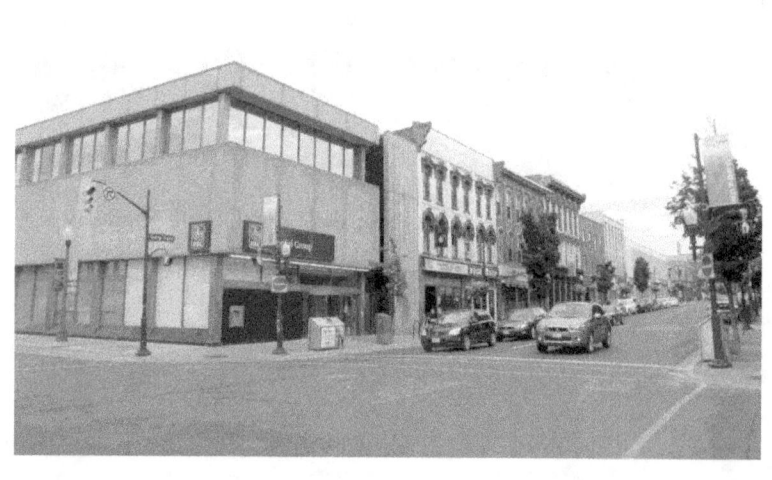

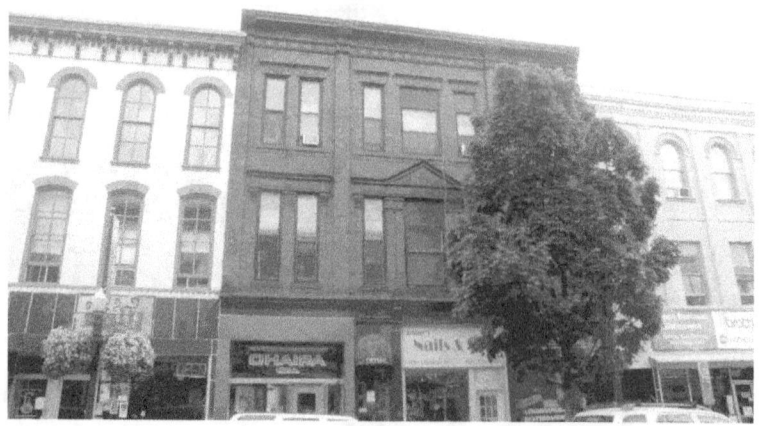

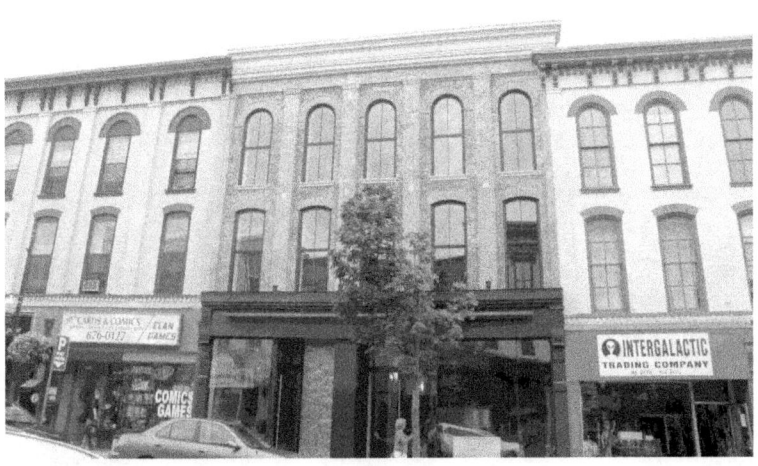

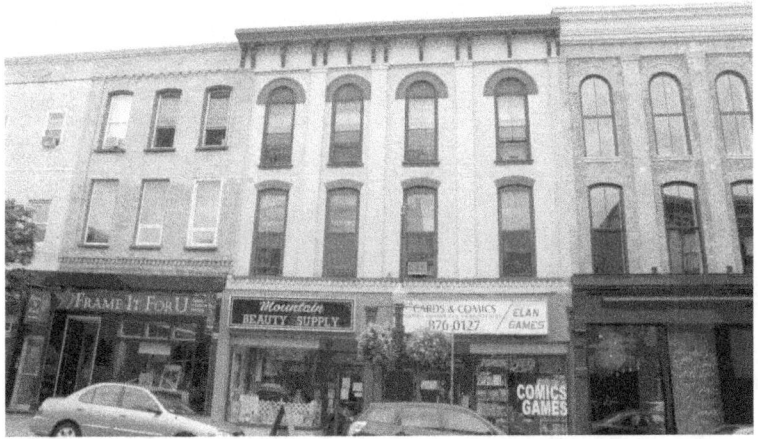

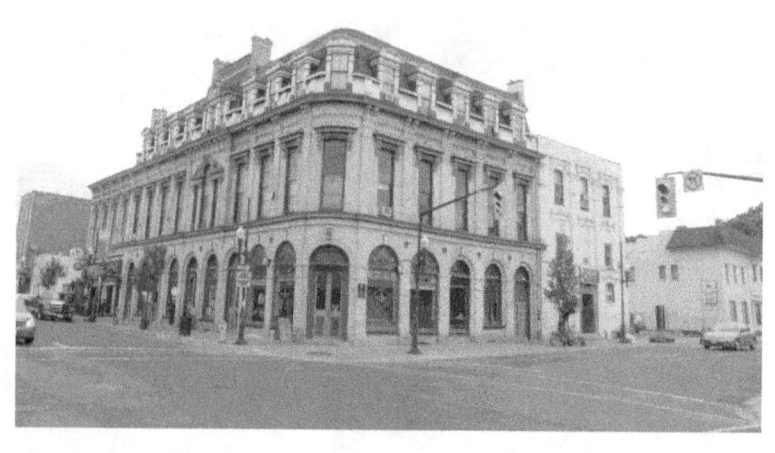

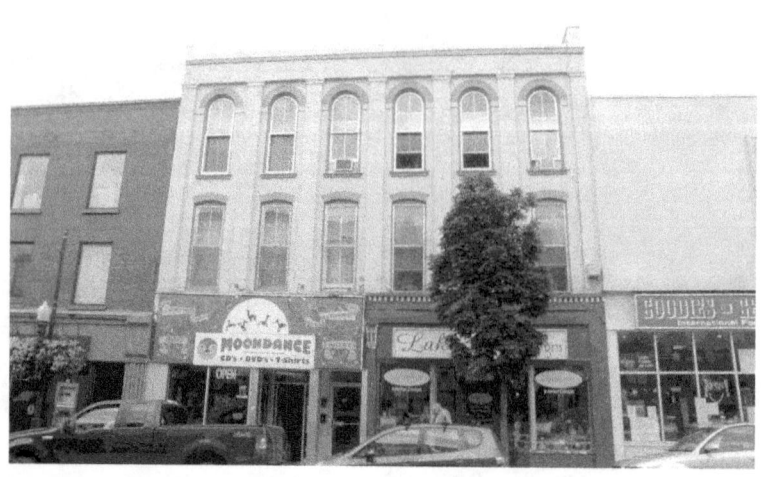

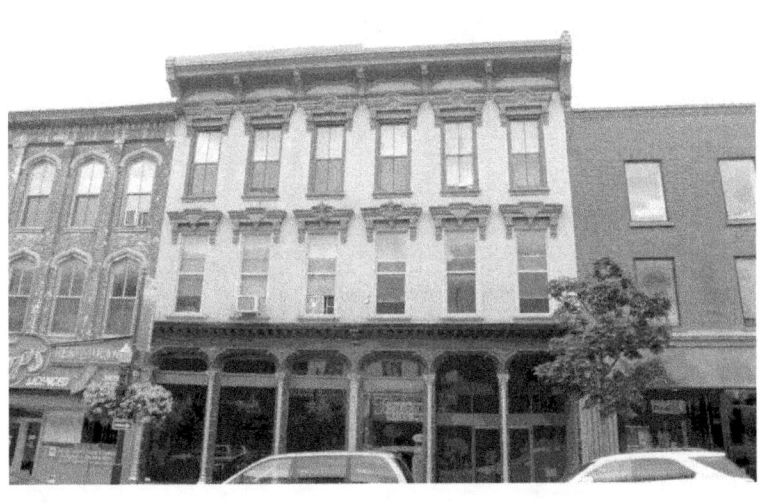

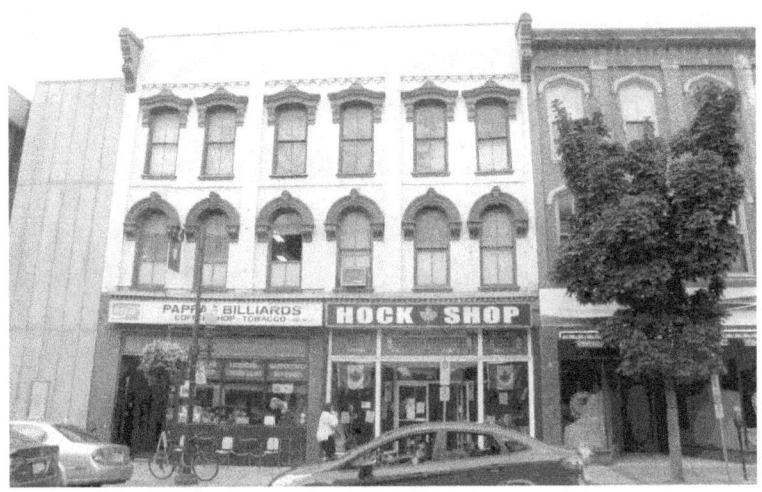

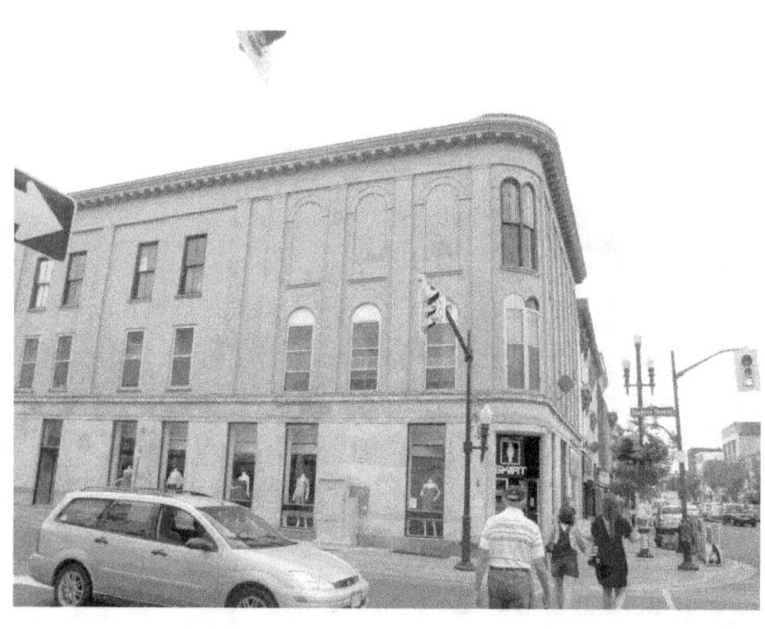

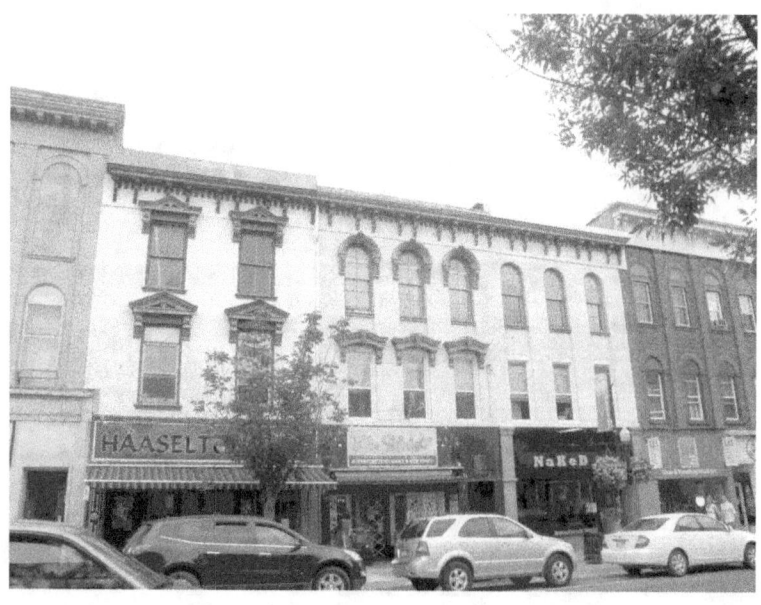

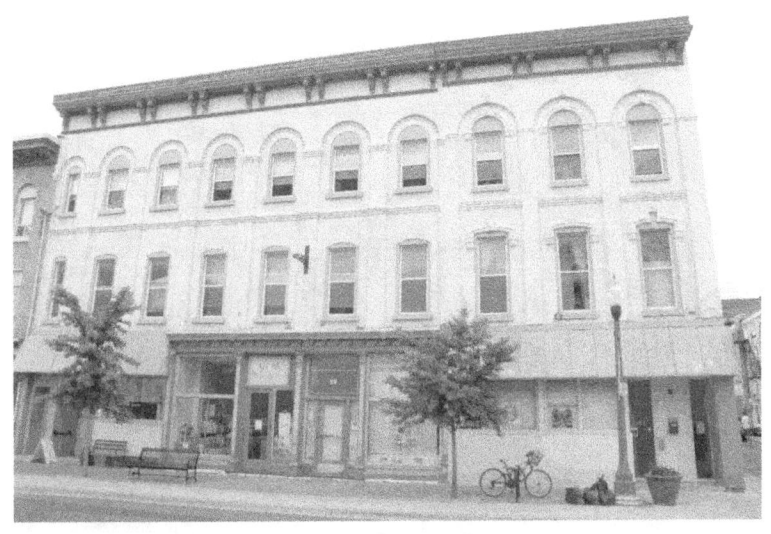

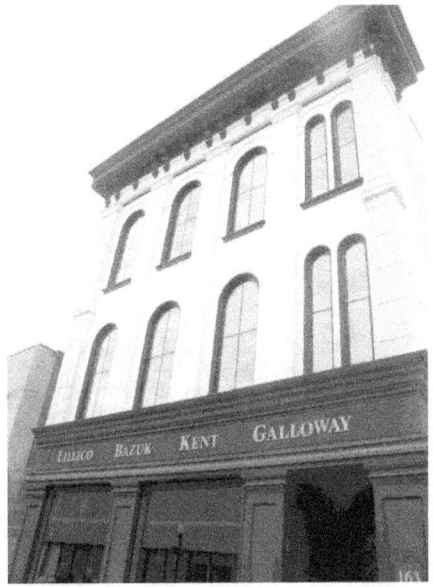

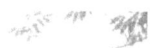

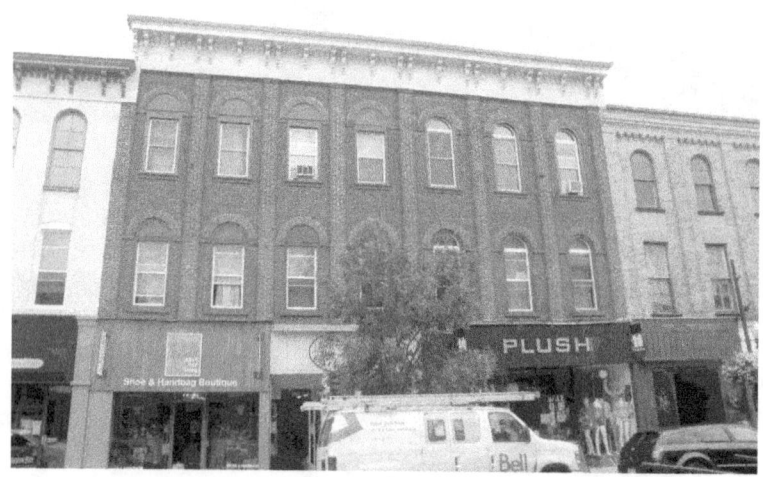

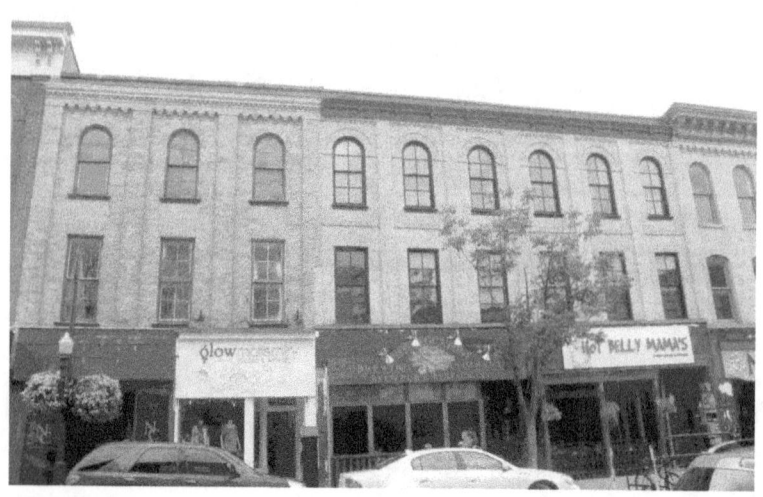

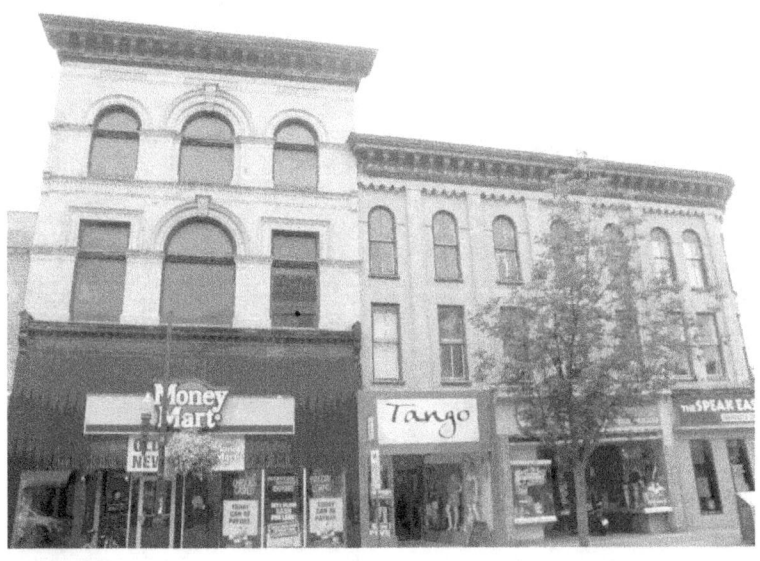

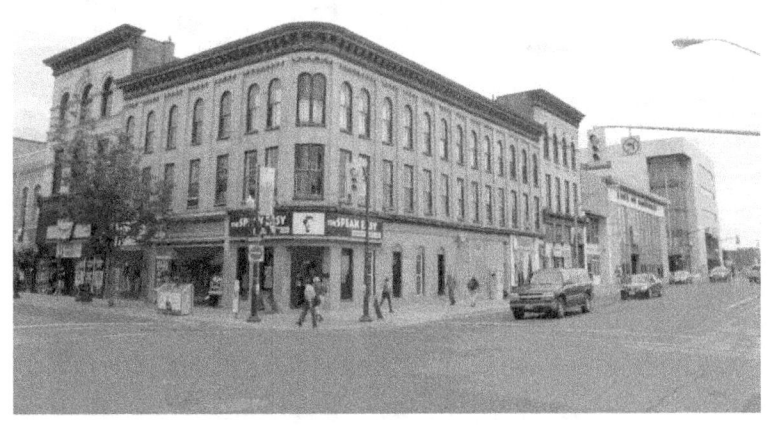

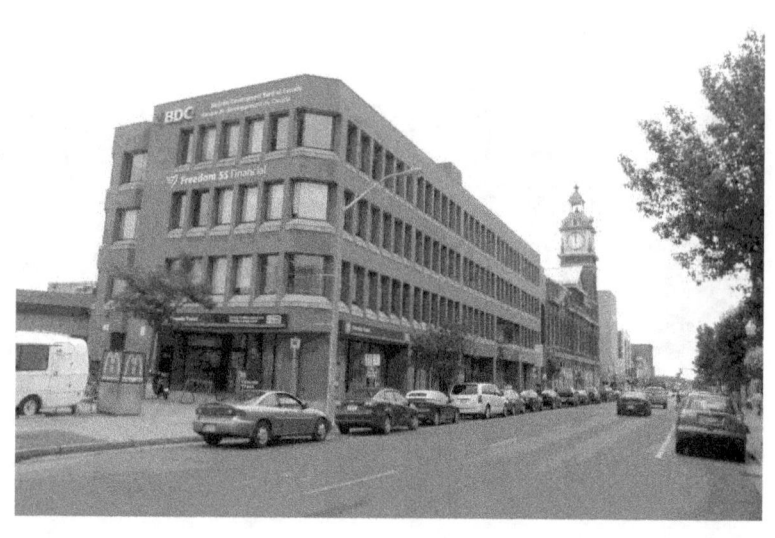

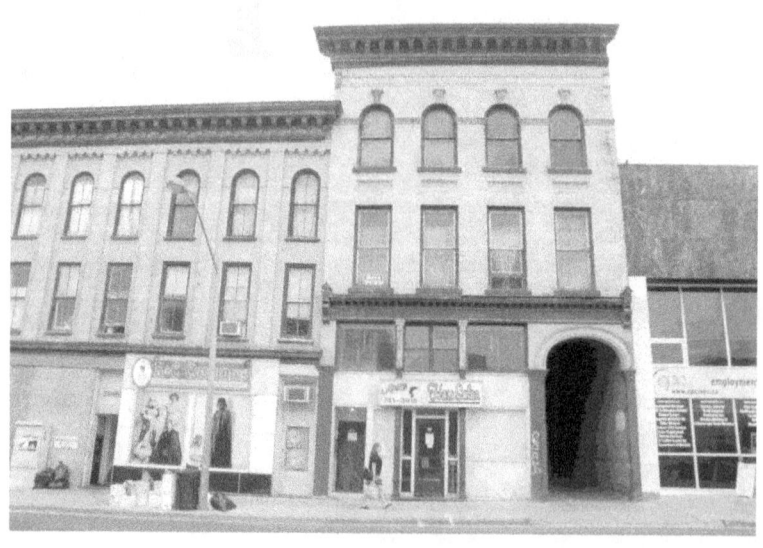

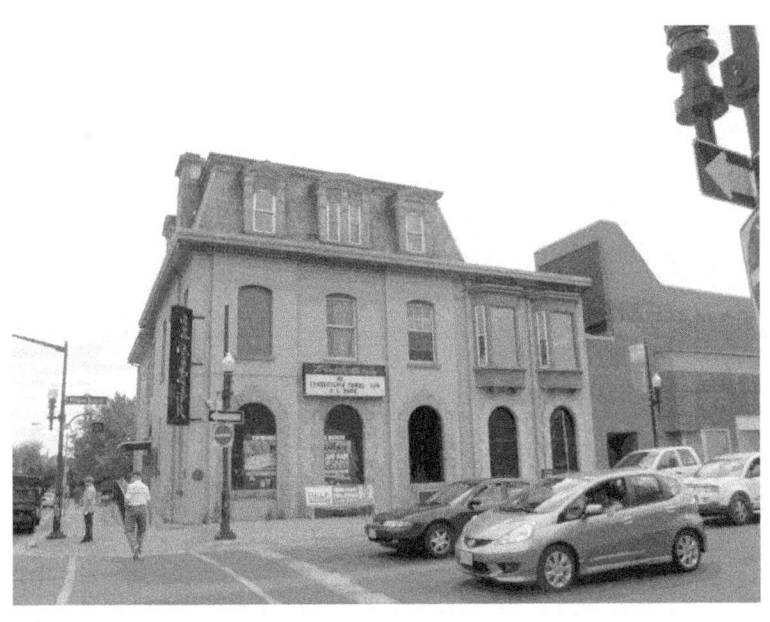

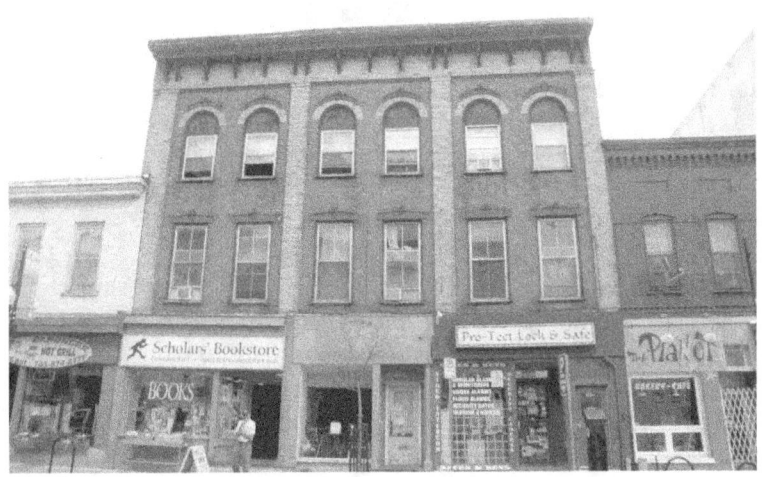

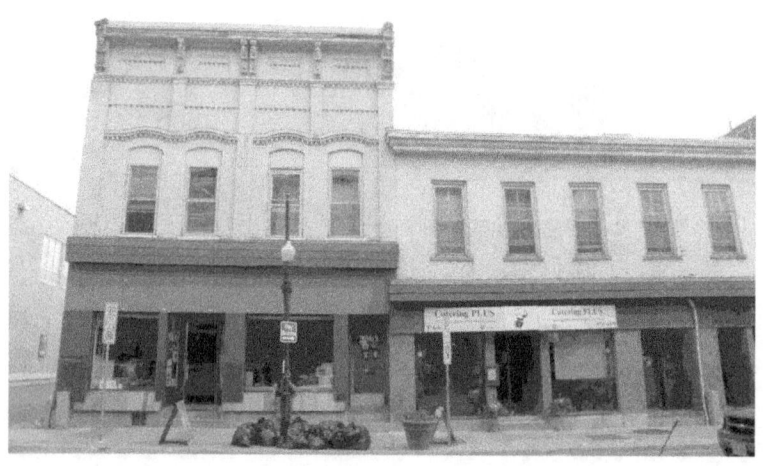

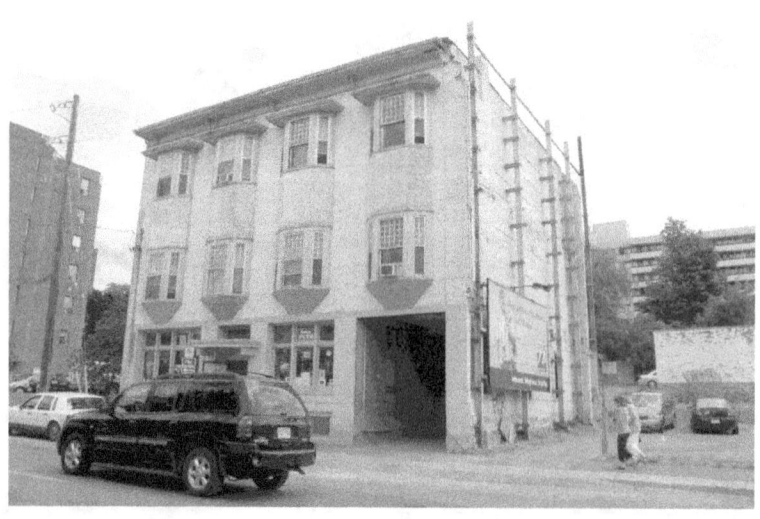

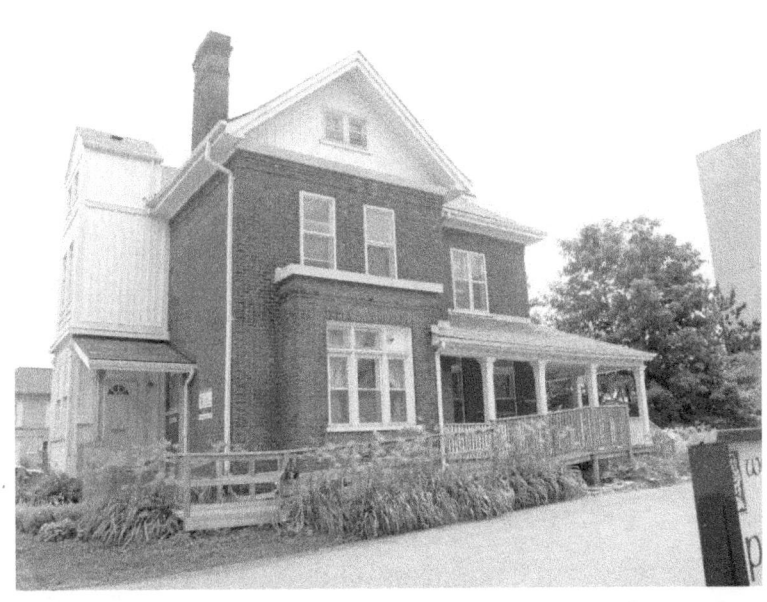

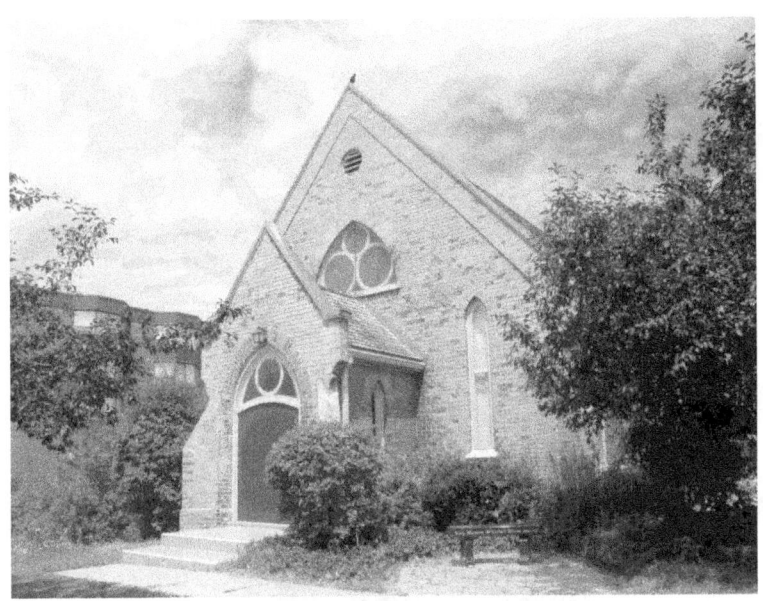

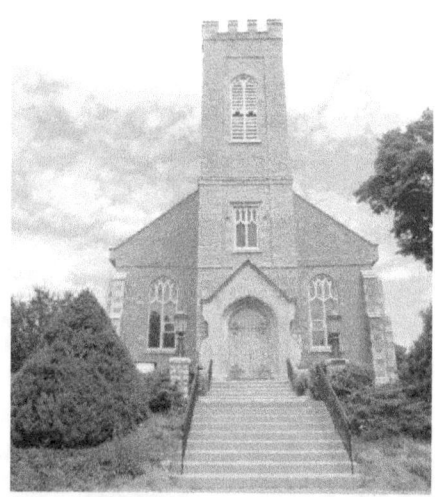

St. John's Anglican Church – established in 1826 – 99 Brock Street. It is Peterborough's oldest church, completed in 1837, in Early English Gothic Revival architecture, in continuous use since its opening.

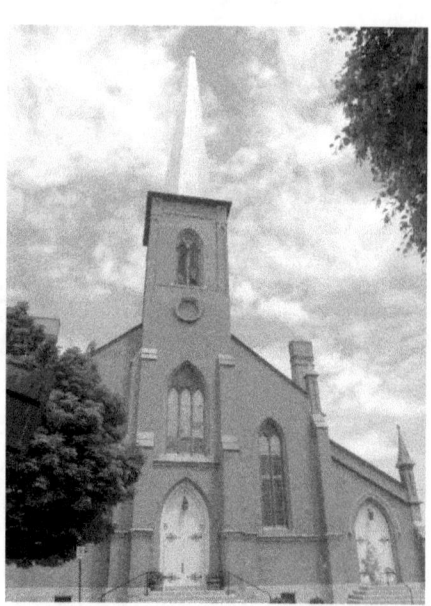

St. Paul's Presbyterian Church, 120 Murray Street

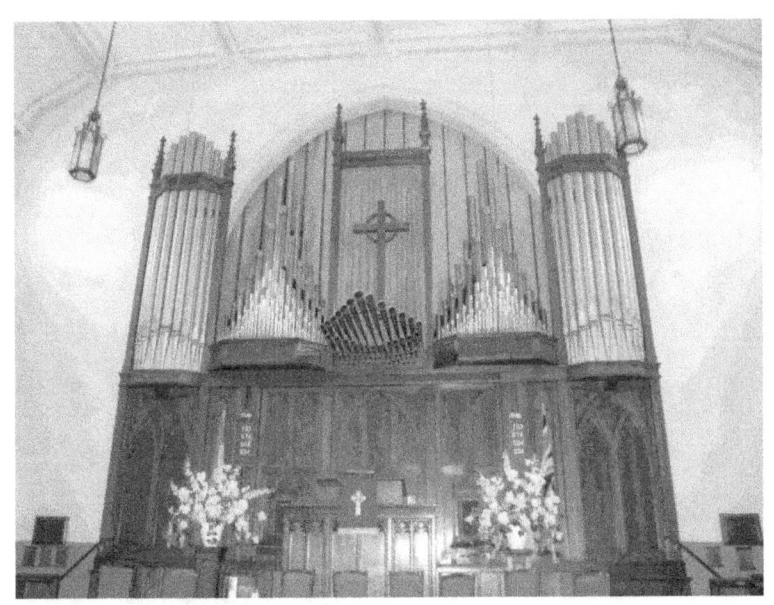

Inside St. Paul's

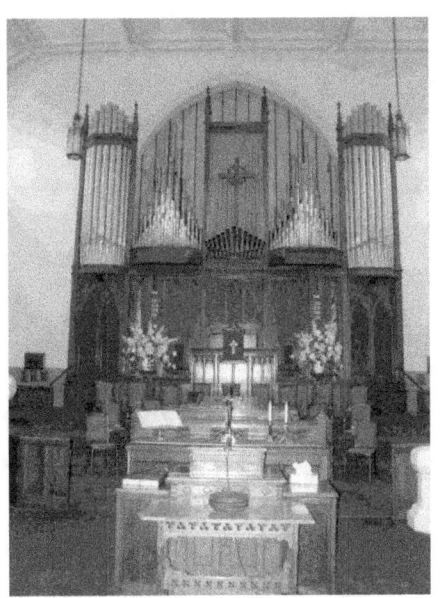

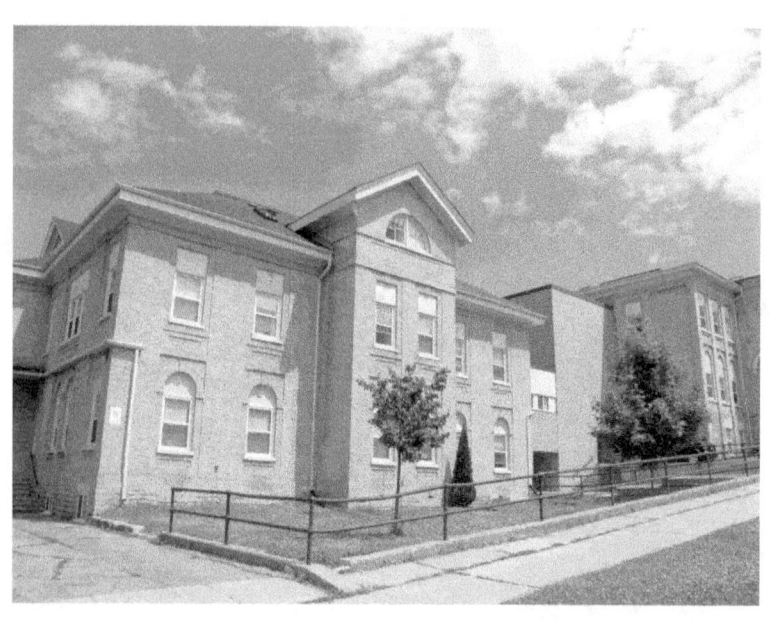

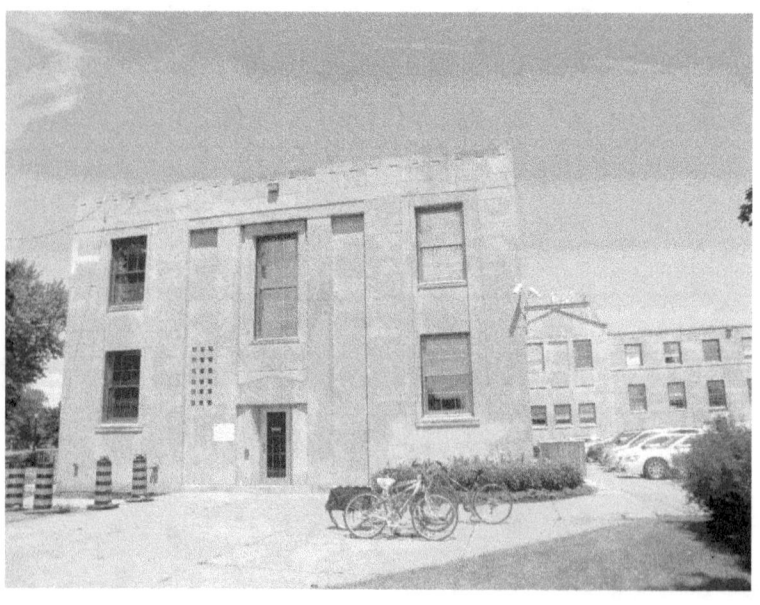

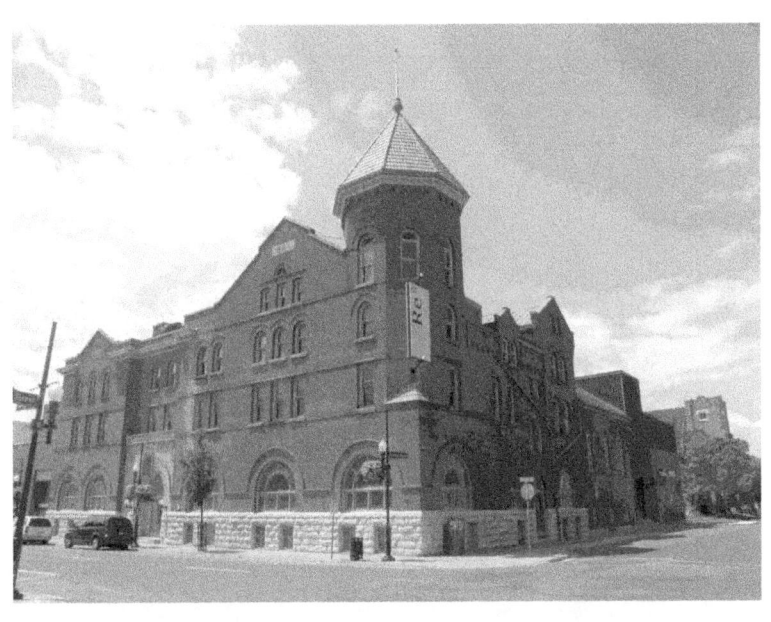

Young Men's Christian Association – 1896

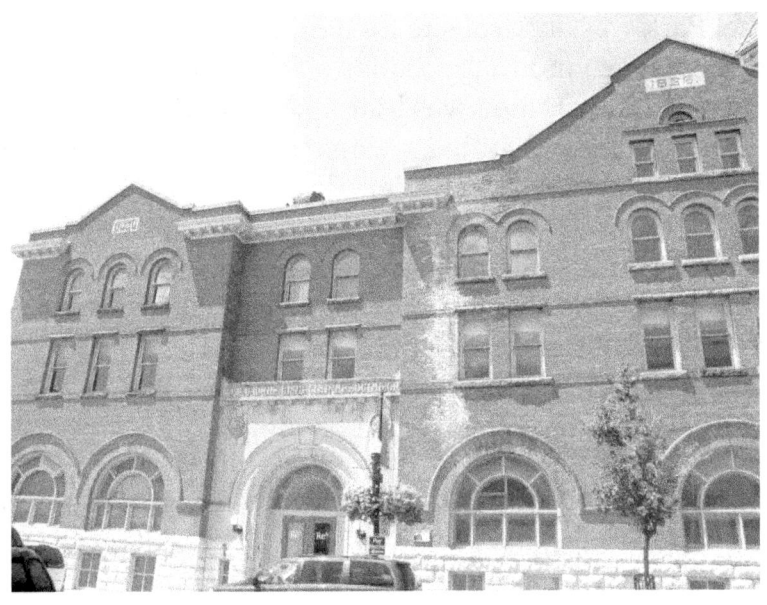

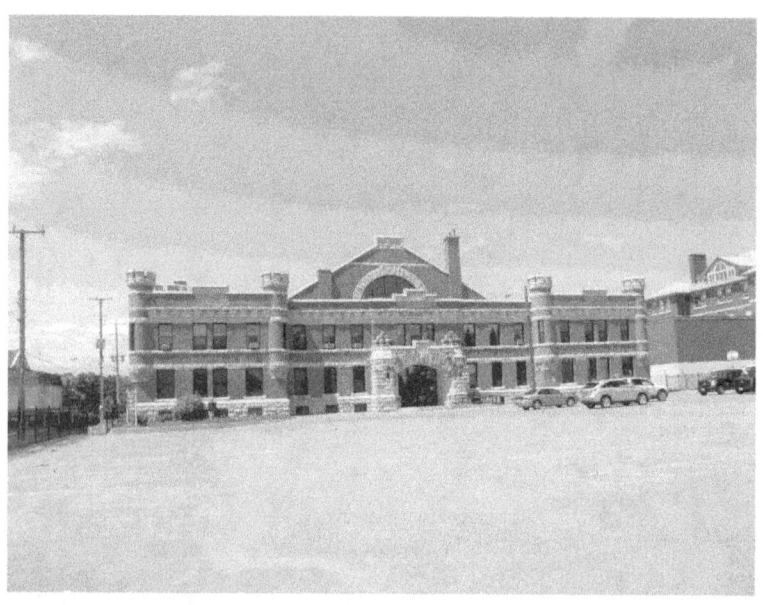

Hastings and Prince Edward Regiment Peterborough Garrison

Central Park was an ideal site for a military training area with its expansive grounds and location – accessible by foot, horse and wagon. A drill shed was built in 1867 and used for bank practices, dances and military activities. Drill sheds were built in many communities across Canada after the Fenian Raids of 1866. The shed was destroyed by fire in 1909, just before the Peterborough Armoury was opened on May 24. The Armoury was built during a nation-wide spending program for the militia in response to the Boer War. The Armoury included a parade hall, living quarters for infantry, cavalry, and artillery, a firing range, and a bowling alley.

The Peterborough Armouries were built in the Romanesque style with turrets, arched troop doors, and crenellated roof line.

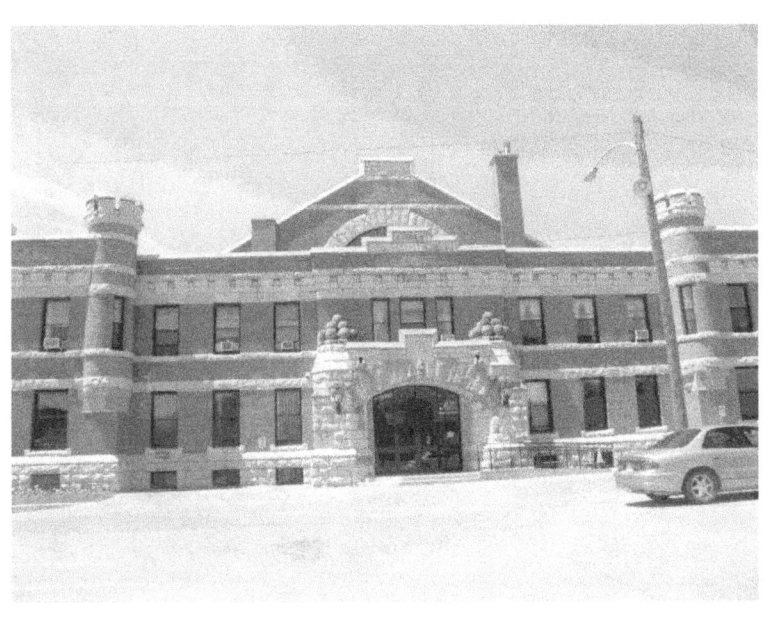

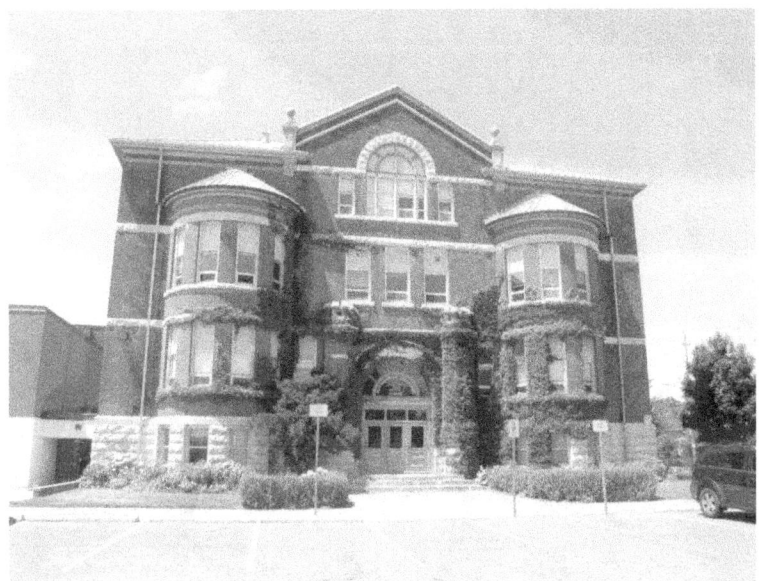

Peterborough Collegiate circa 1917 – McDonnel Street
Romanesque Revival architecture

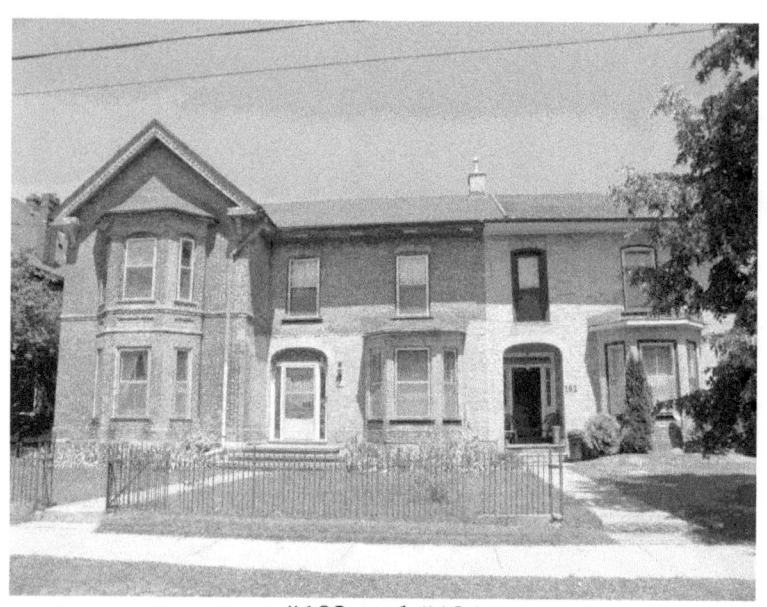

#192 and #194

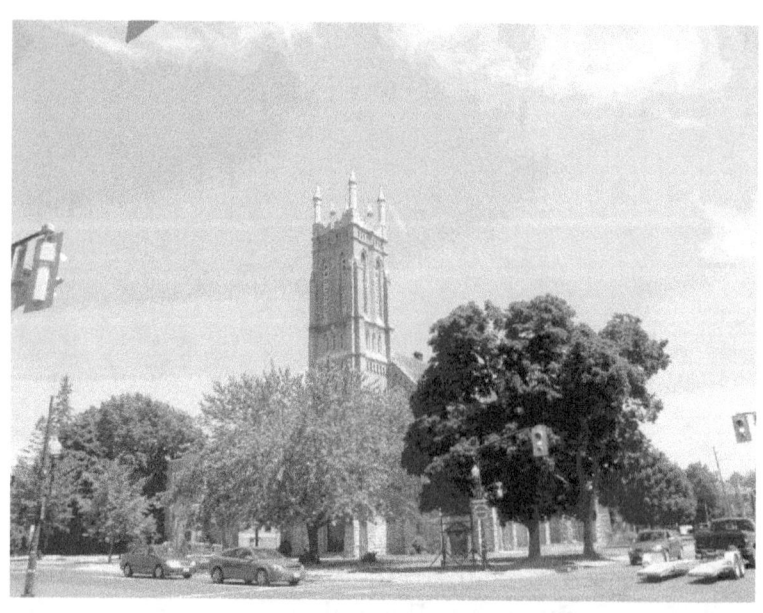

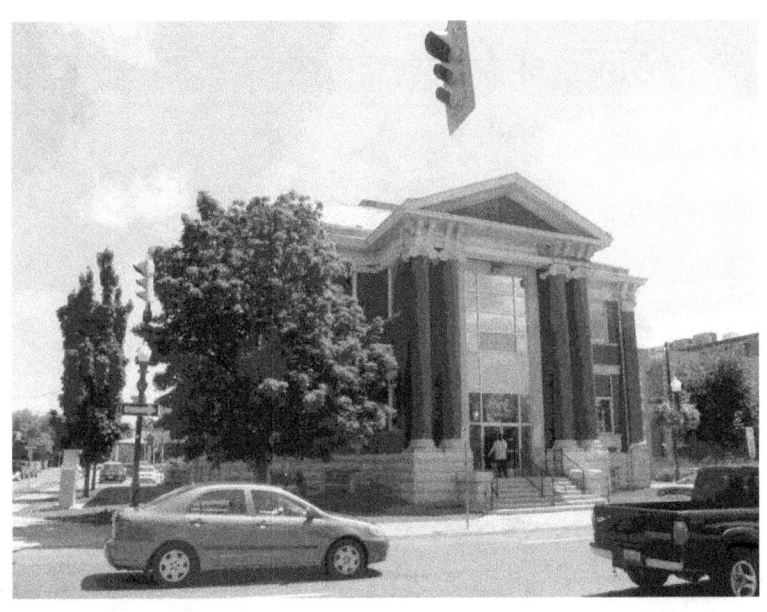

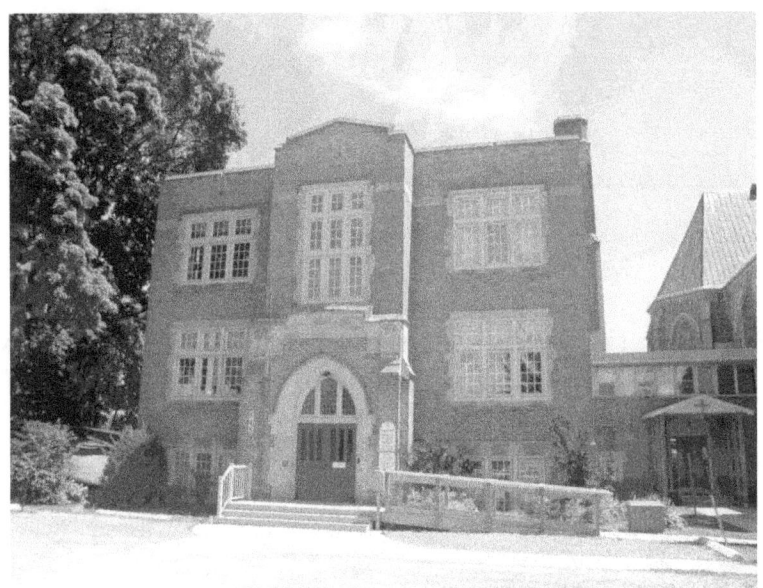

George Street United Church, 540 George Street

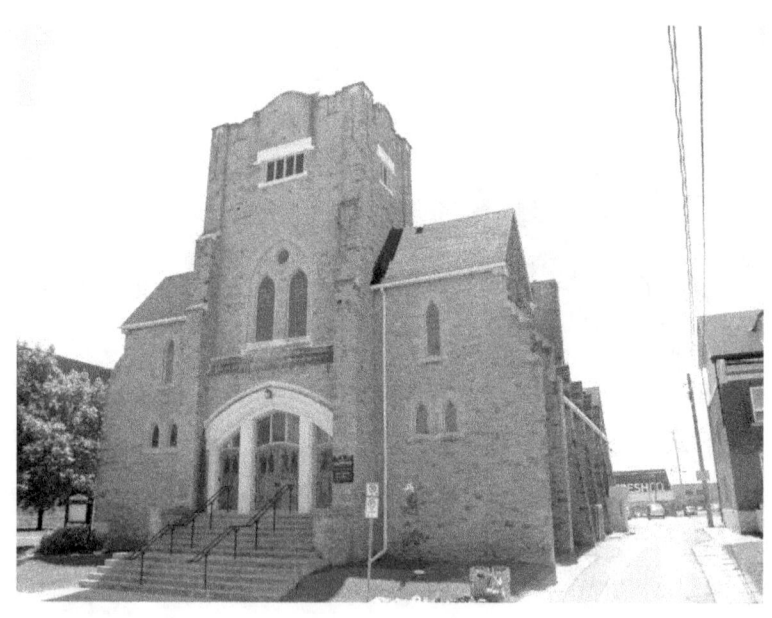

Baptist Church

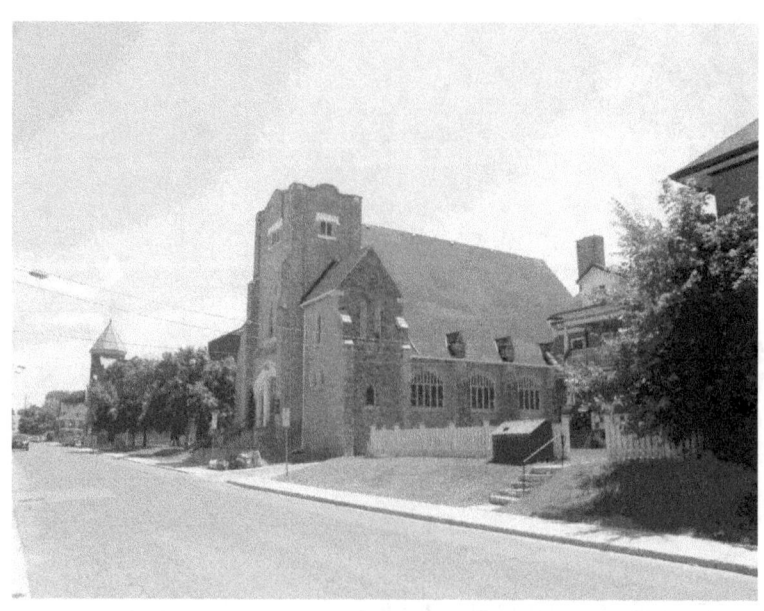

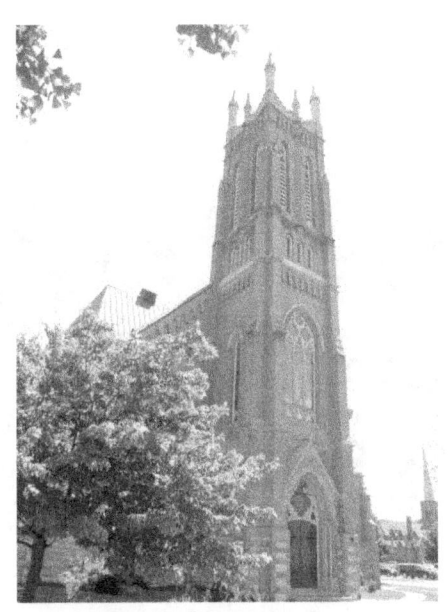

1875 Wesleyan Methodist Church

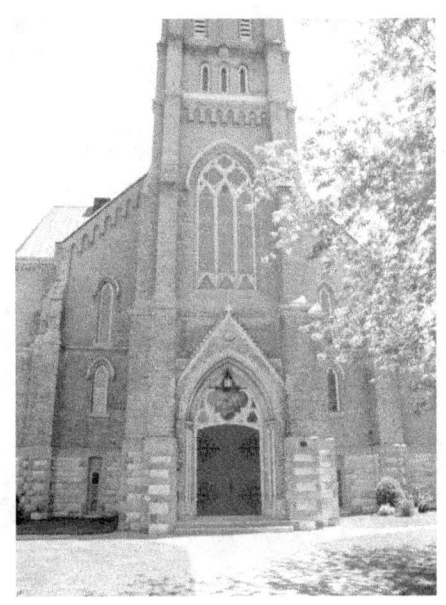

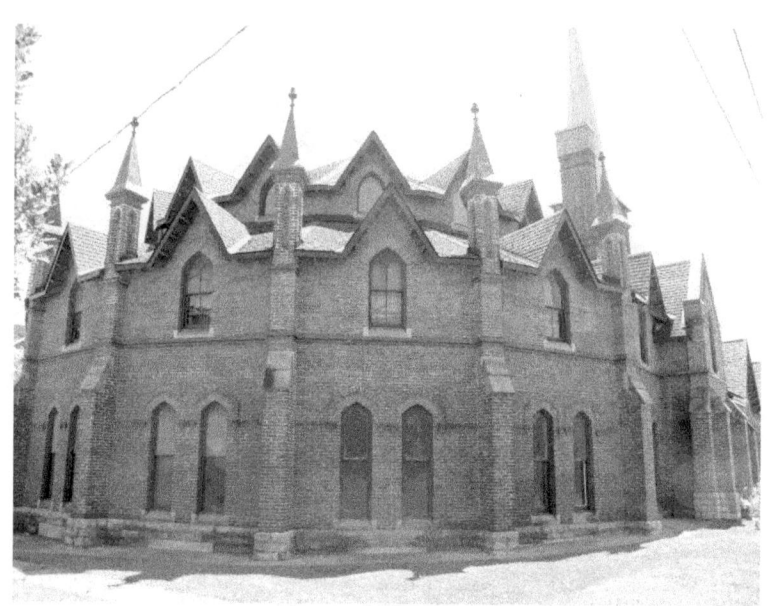

Police

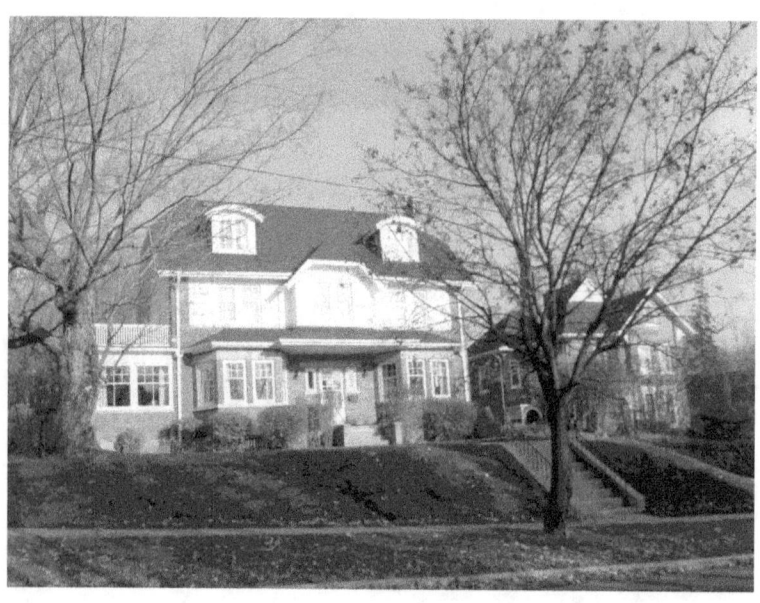

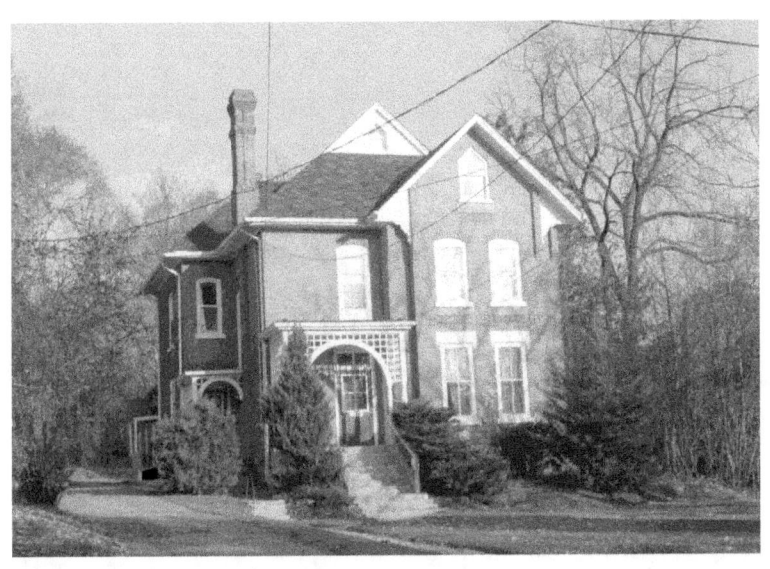

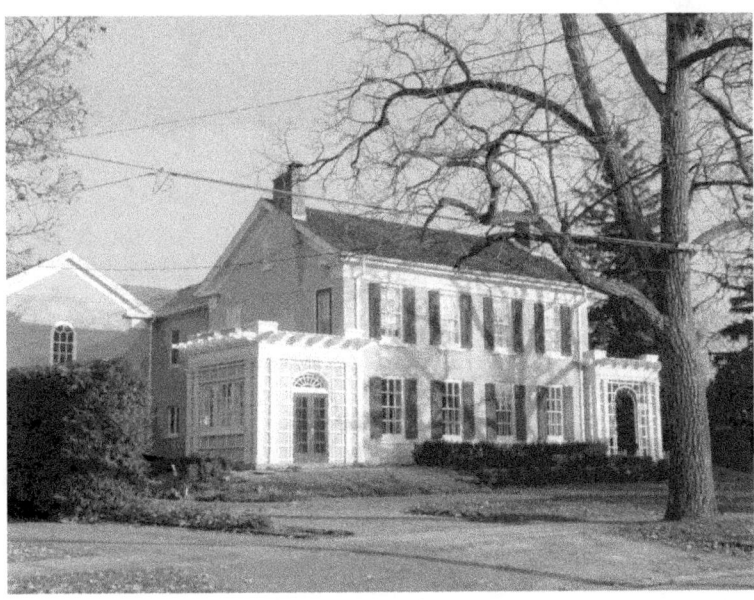

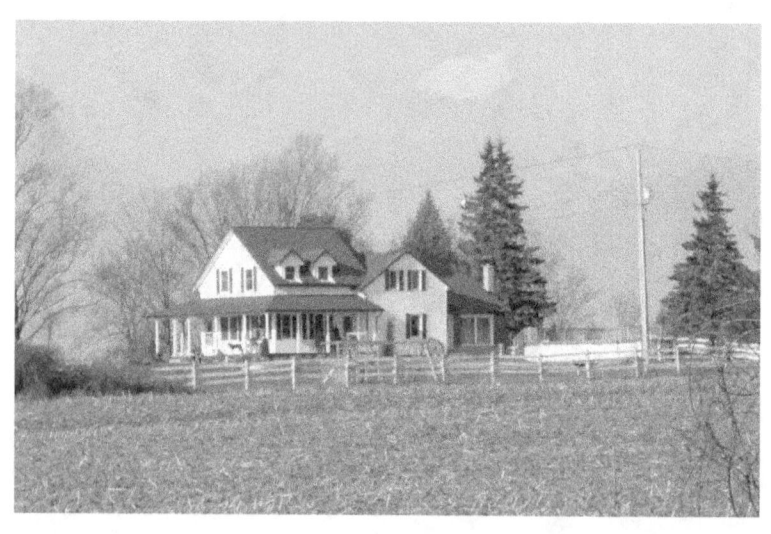

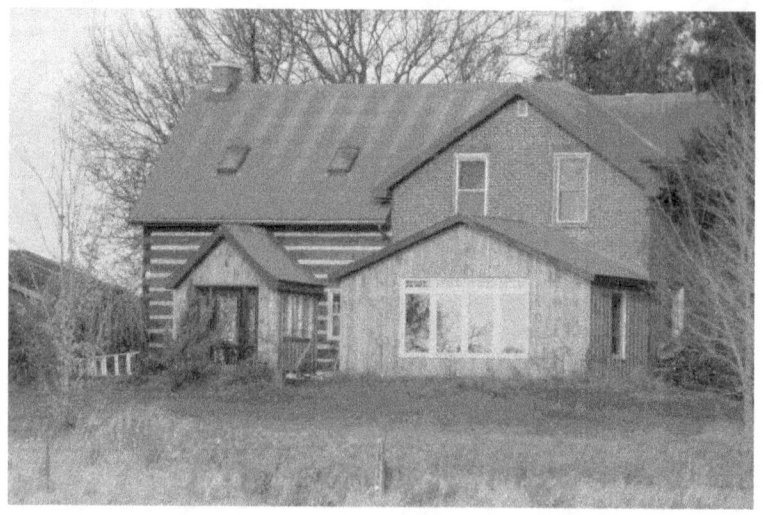

Bridgenorth

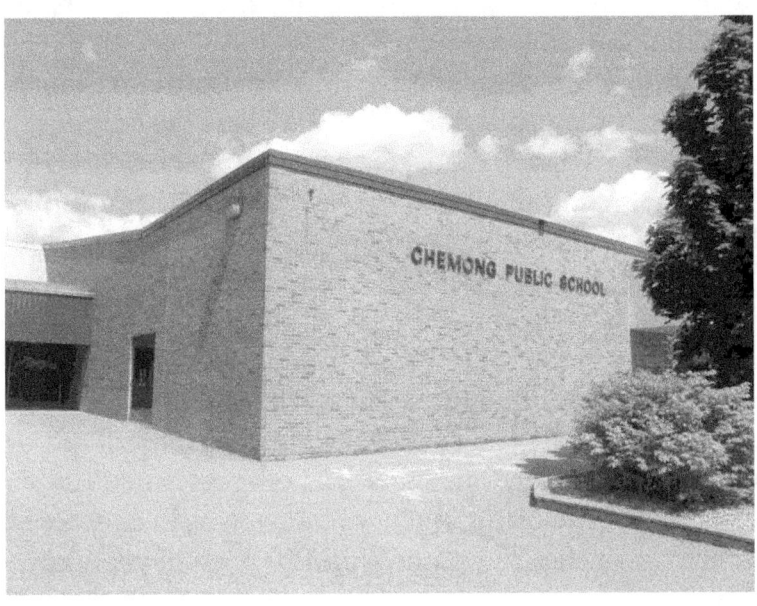

Chemong Public School with mural of original school

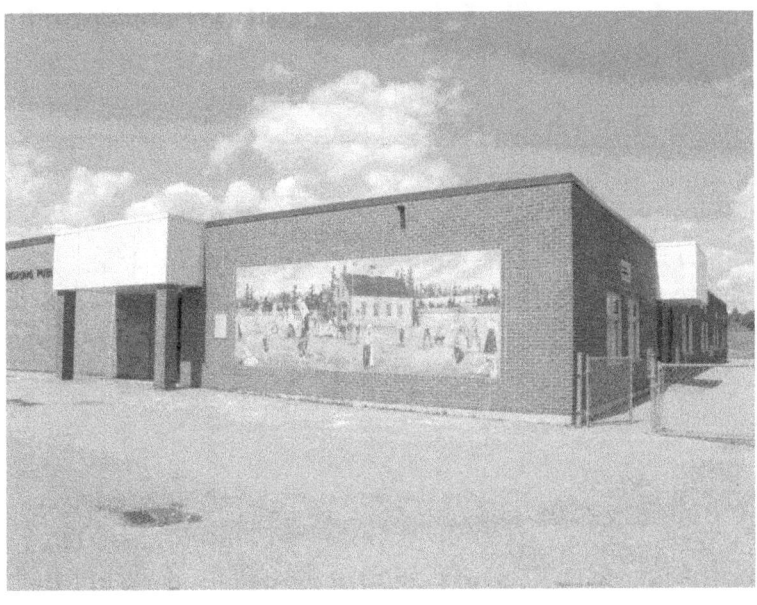

The red brick school house was a focal point in many nineteenth century Ontario communities. Smith Township was divided into seven school districts in 1873, with the Bridgenorth section named #5. The school property on Colborne Street was purchased for $125 and the school building with two water closets and a wood shed cost $1,025. S.S. No. 5 was completed in August 1876. The community held a picnic to celebrate the opening.

For many years, children living in school section #5 attended the one room school house for all grades, receiving an education typical of the time. The mid-twentieth century saw expansion of the original school, and the opening of the Gore Street site, and resulted in S.S. No. 5 being renamed Chemong Public School. The original school house was in use continually as a classroom until June 2002 – 126 years of learning.

Richard Hayman, Director of the Art School of Peterborough, was commissioned by Chemong School Council to paint the mural during the summer of 2002 to honour the little red school house that so many children have attended. Assisted by artist Donna Bolam, Richard has created an imaginative portrayal of recess circa 1876.

Students at Chemong modeled for the mural in 2002. They are all descendants of original Bridgenorth area families. Old family names represented include Bell, Jopling, Kelly, Mann, McIlmoyle, McManus, McWilliams, Nichols, Northey, Robinson, and Wood.

The mural was unveiled at the opening of the primary addition of Chemong Public School on October 2, 2002. The community spirit of the one room school will live on in Bridgenorth.

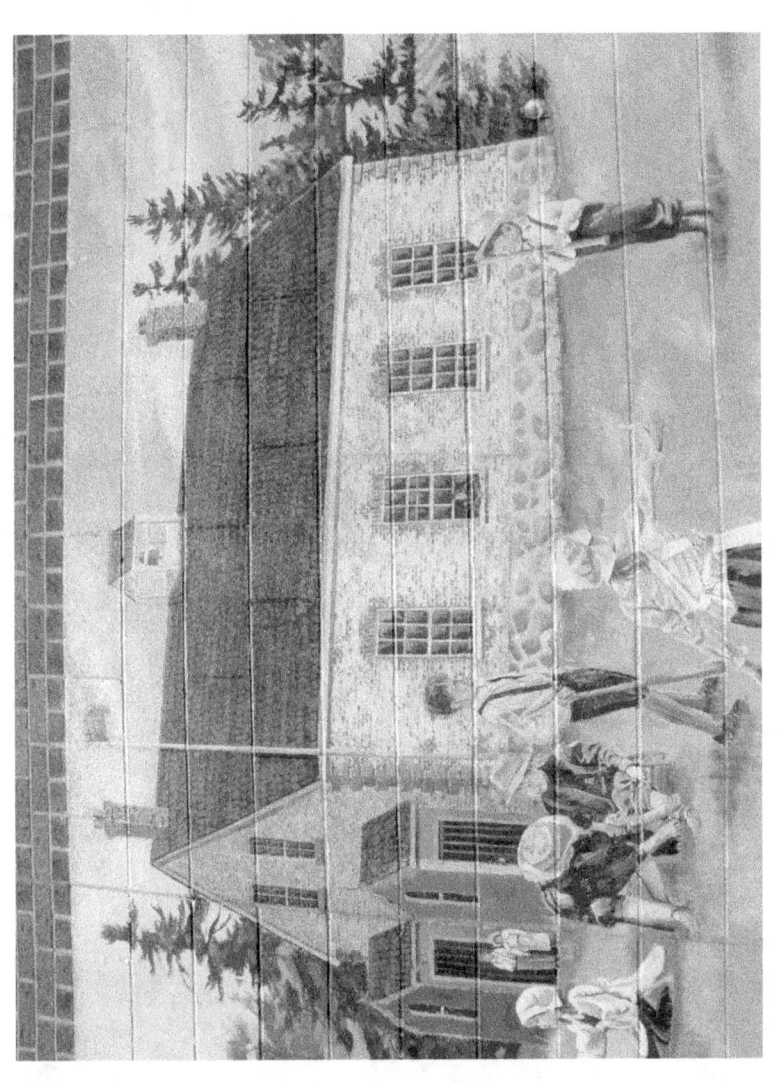

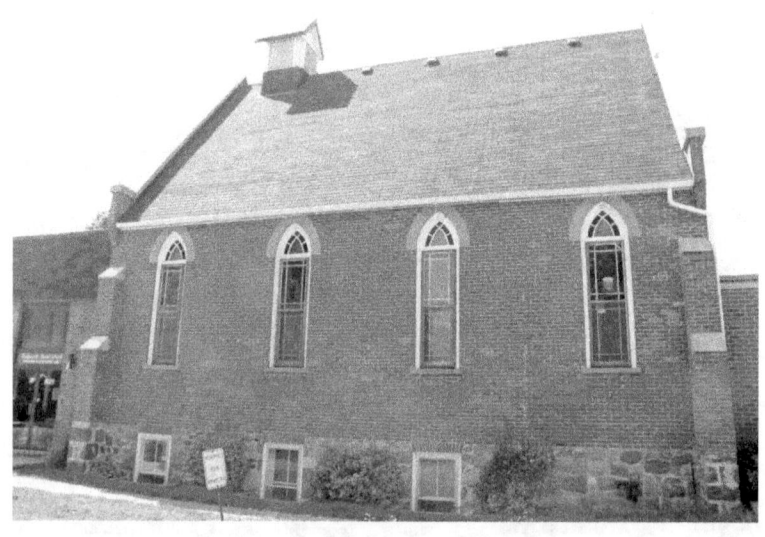

Bridgenorth United Church, founded 1842, erected 1889

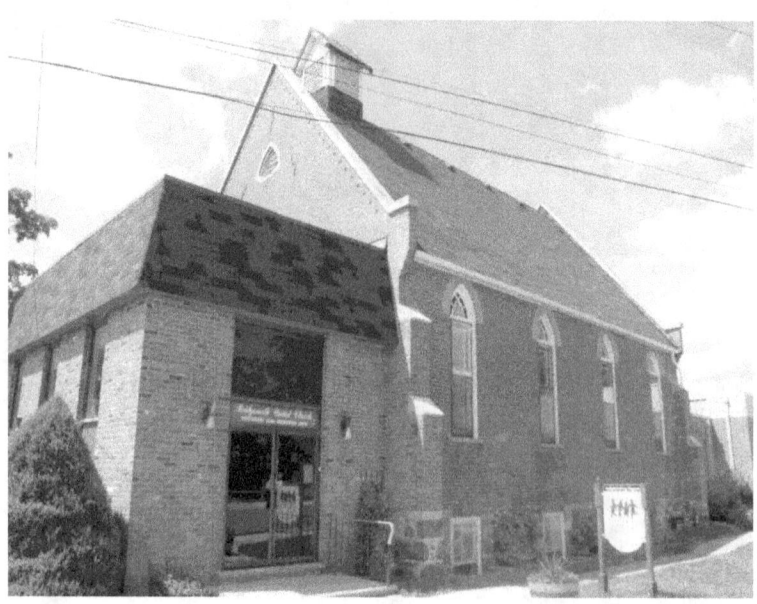

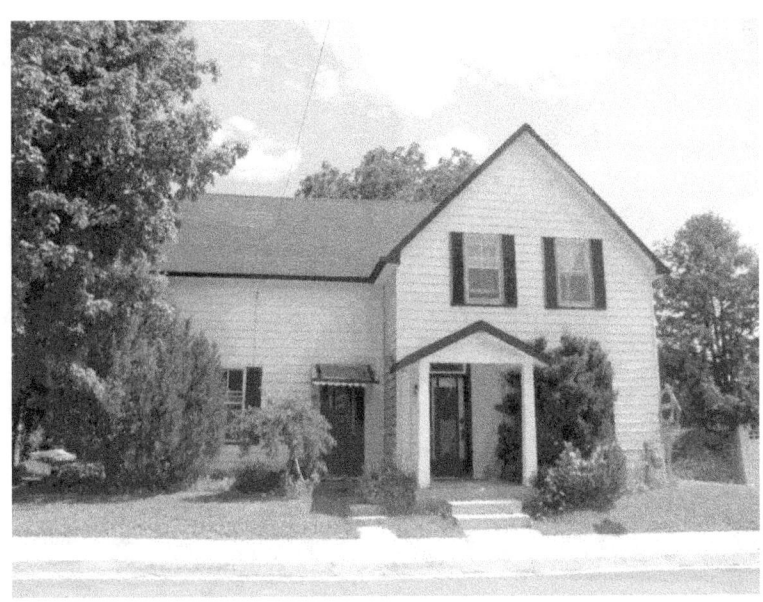

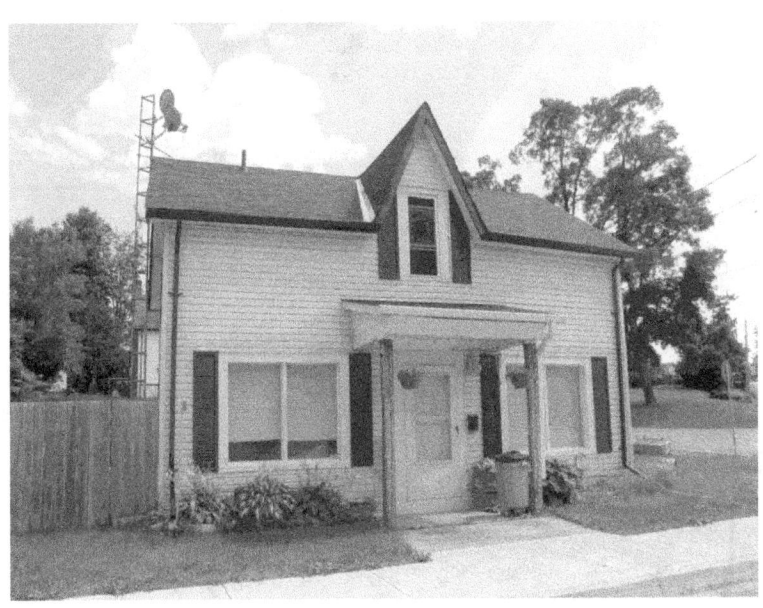

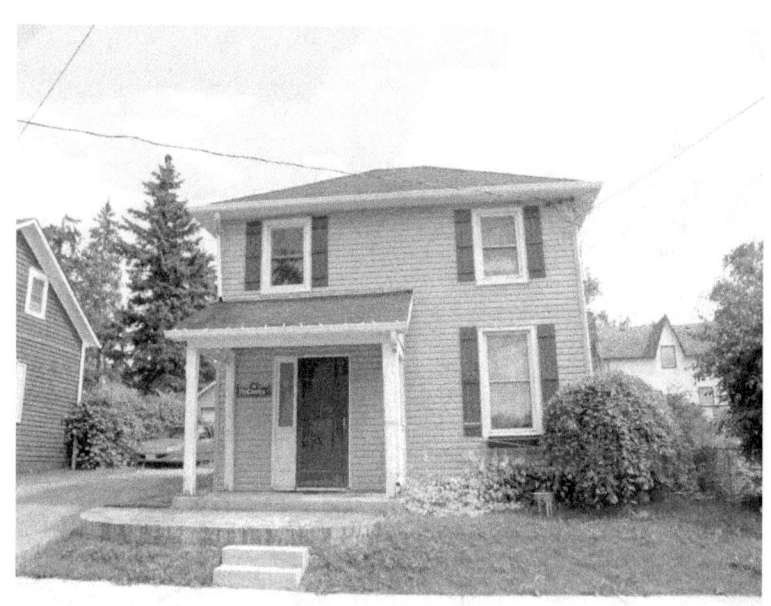

799 Charles Street

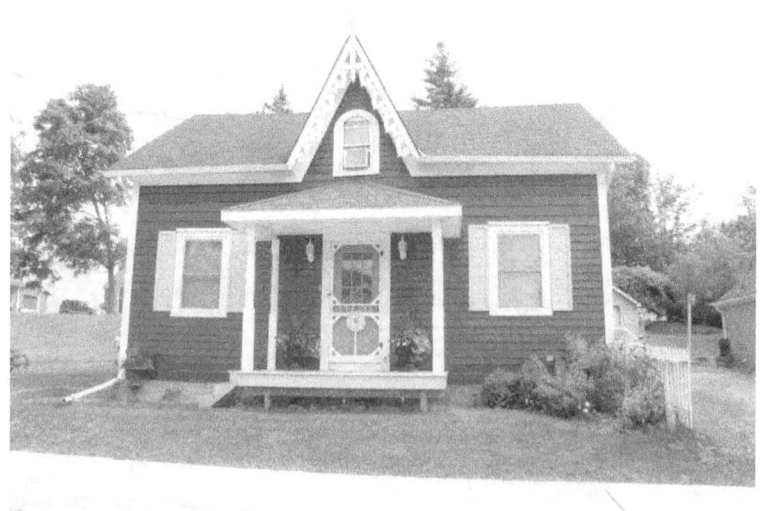

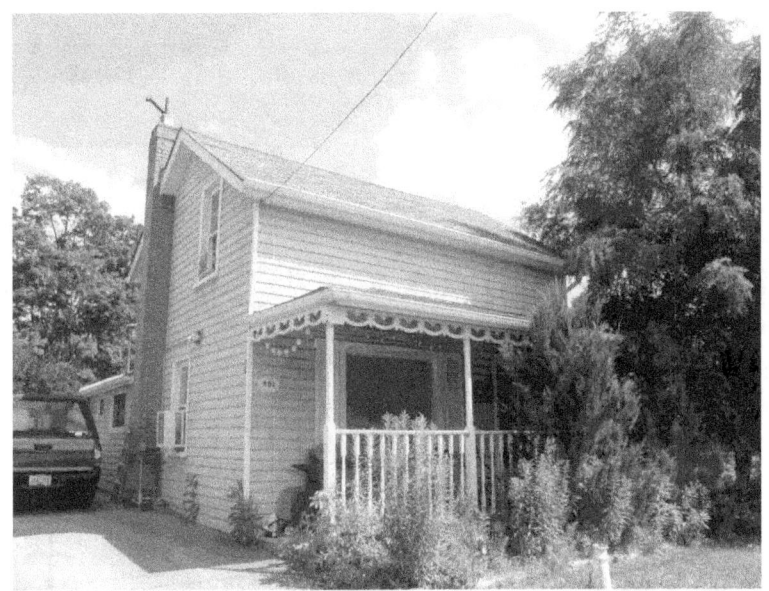

801

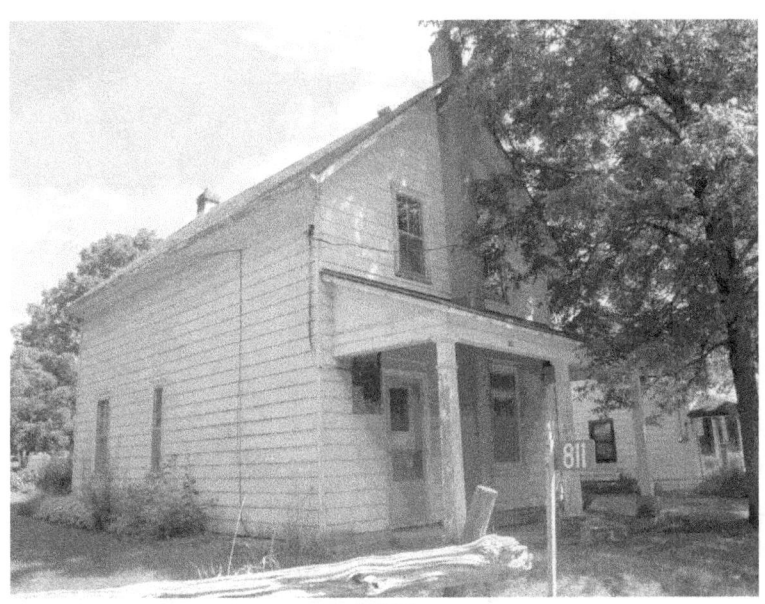

#811

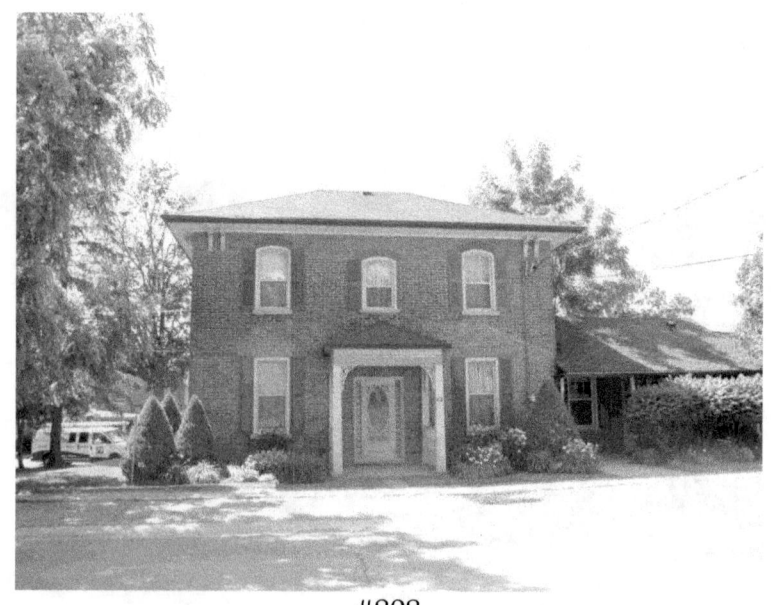

#808

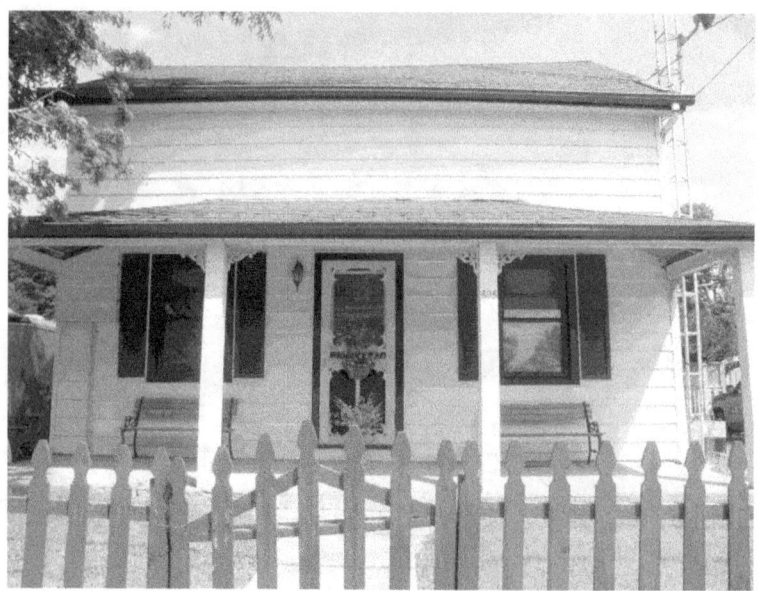

#805

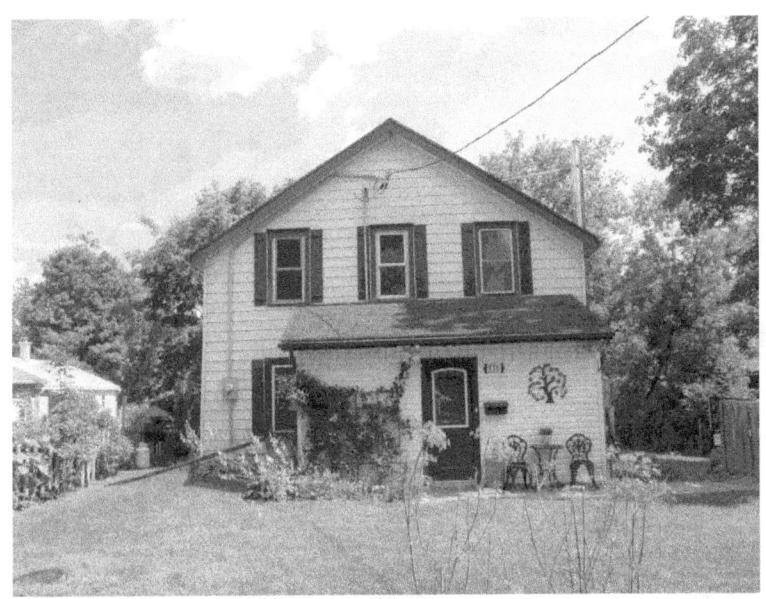

#751

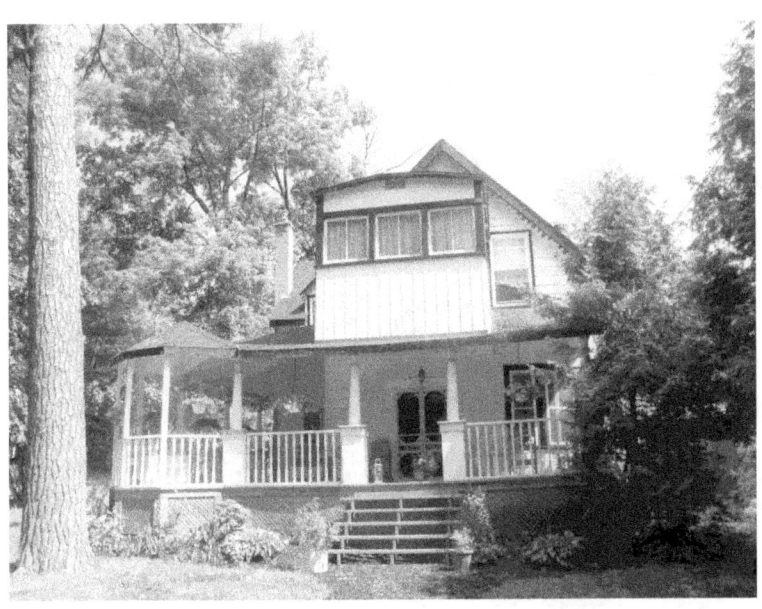

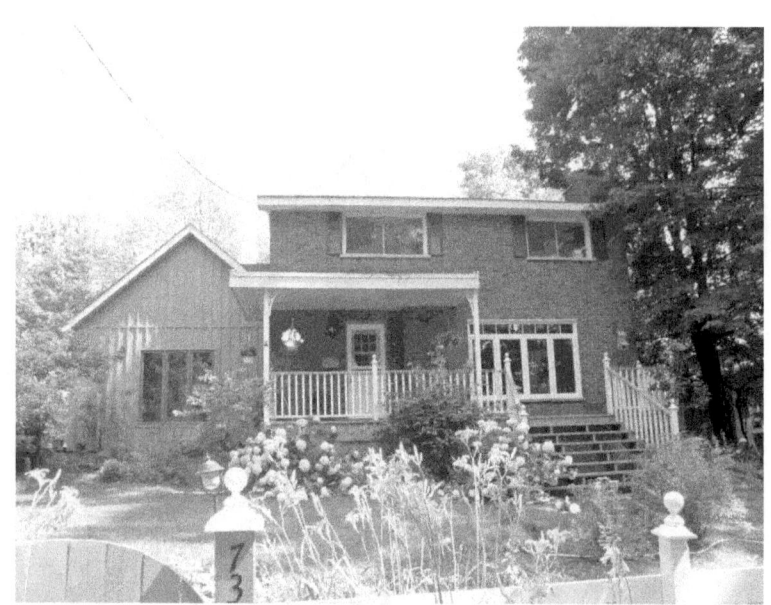

#73_

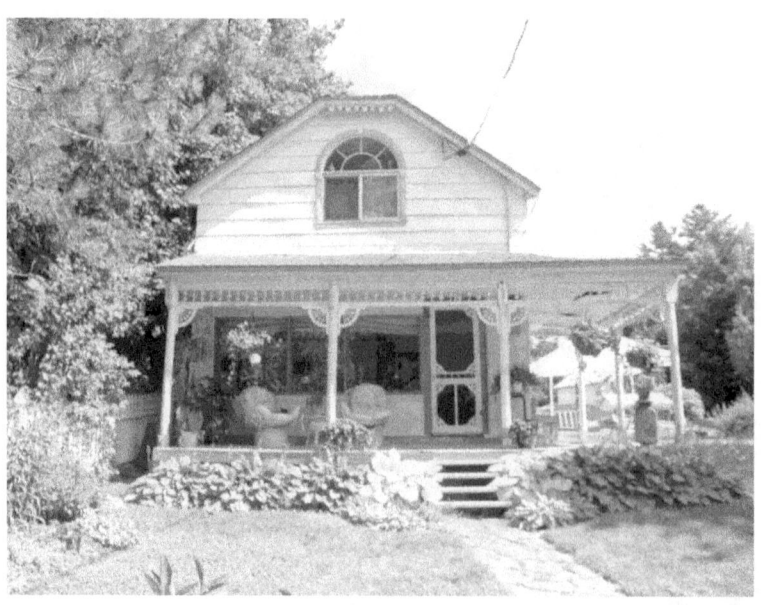

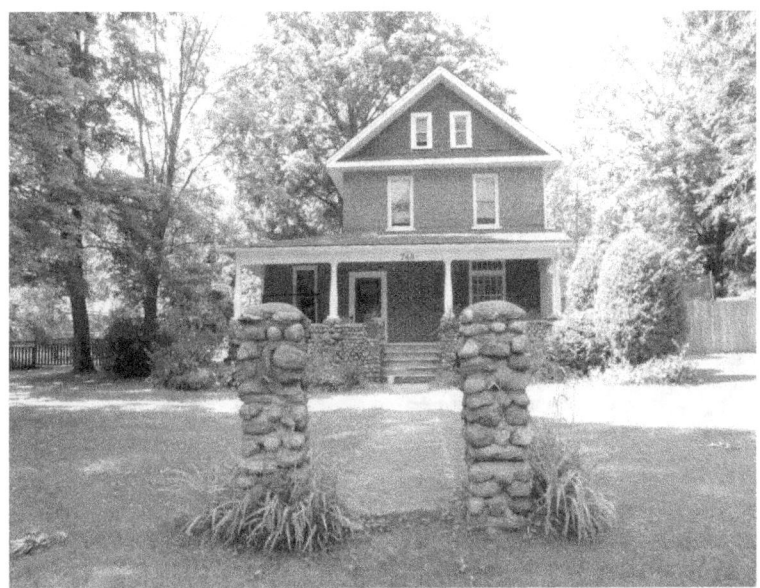

#748

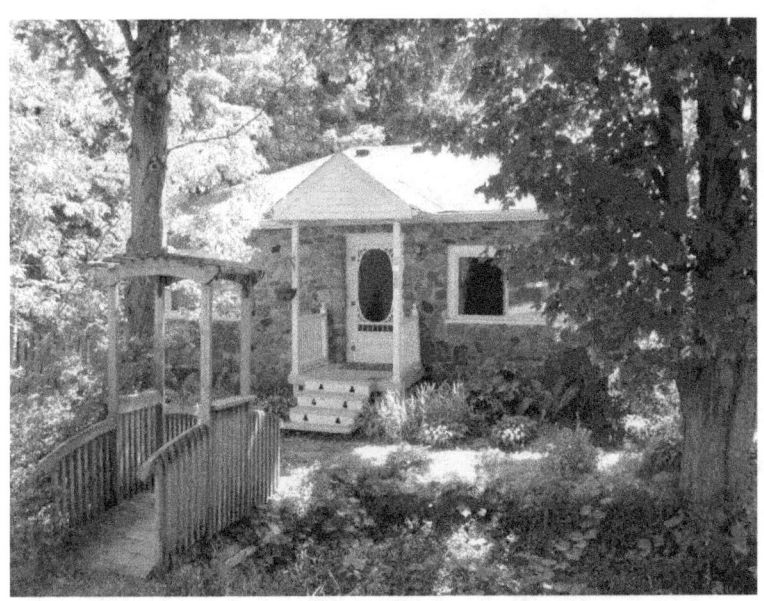

Emerald Isle

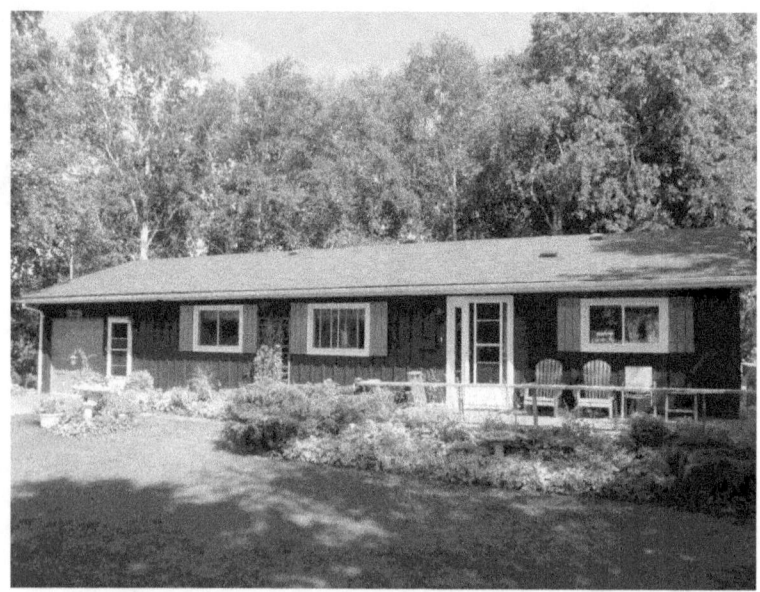

Home of Art and Iris Frankum, Cow Island

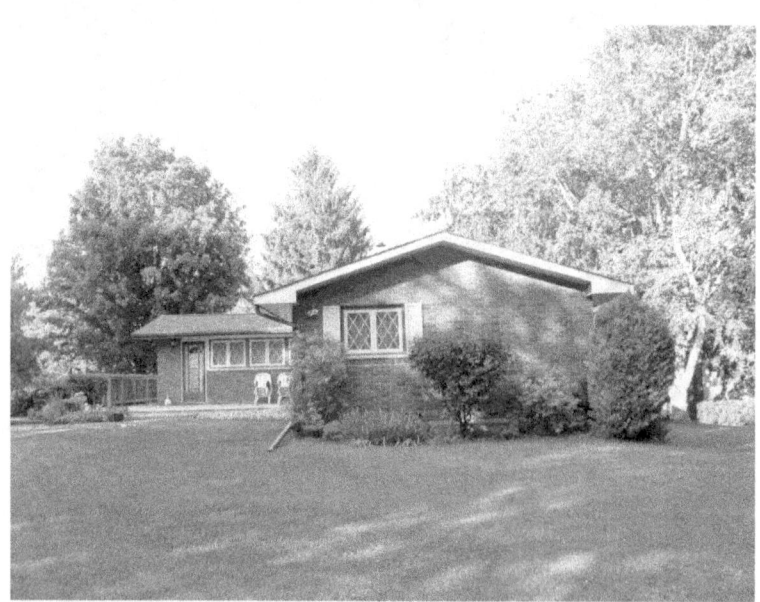

Where Art and Iris Frankum lived from 1967-1980

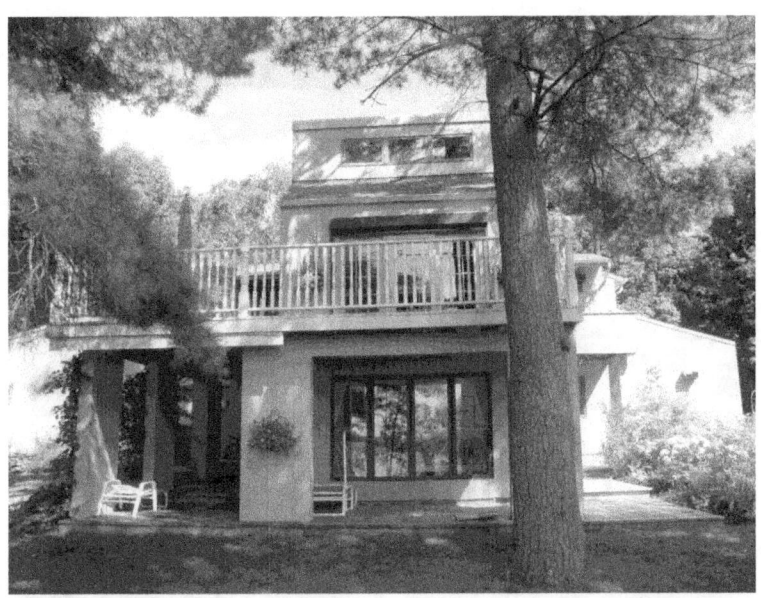

View from water of Harry and Pat Burton's home on
Buckhorn Lake

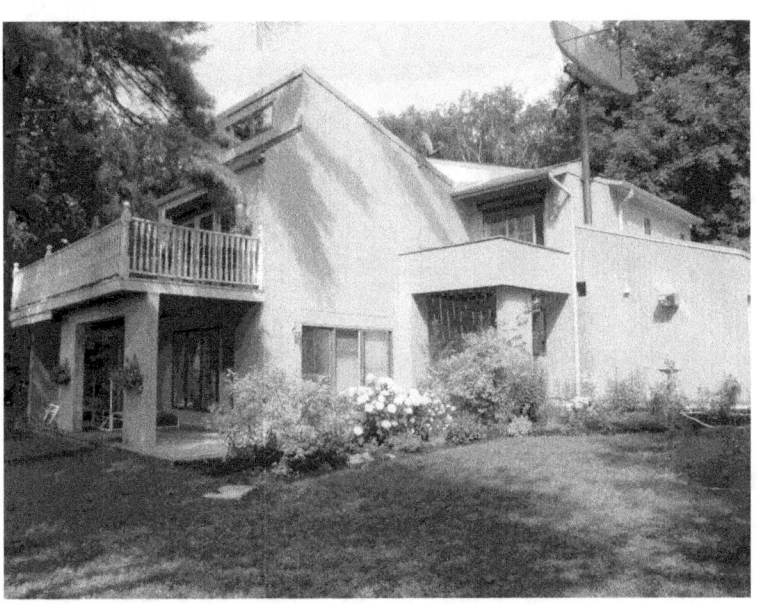

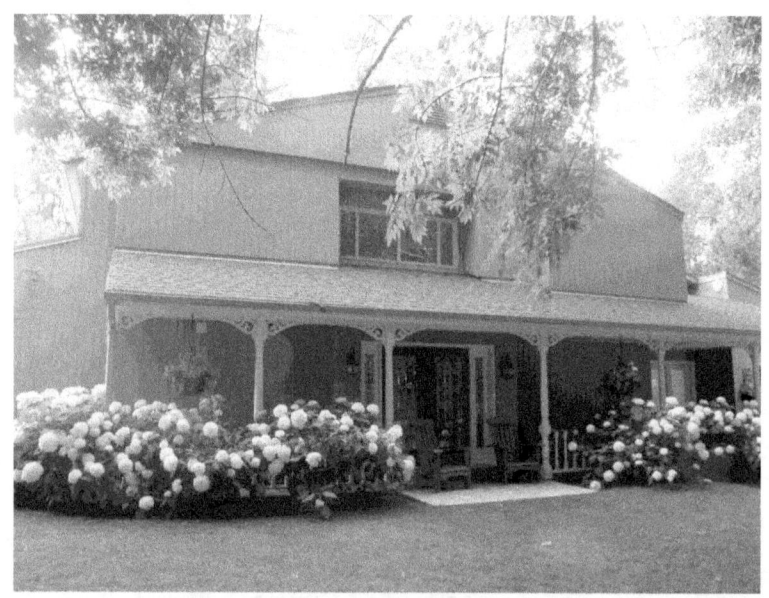

View of Pat and Harry's house

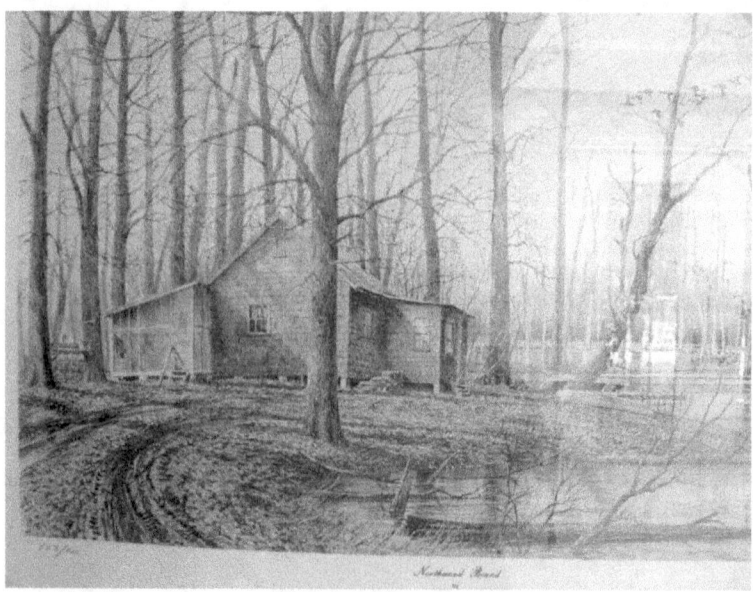

Like Burton's cottage before the house was built

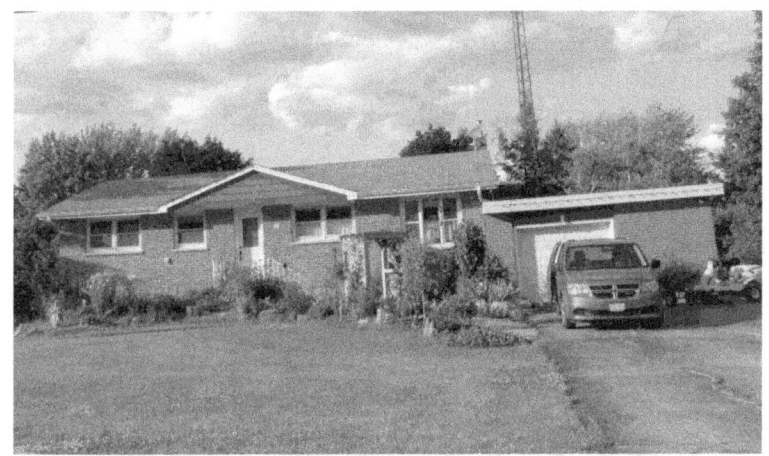

Steve and Bonnie Feeney's house where Brad Feeney lives

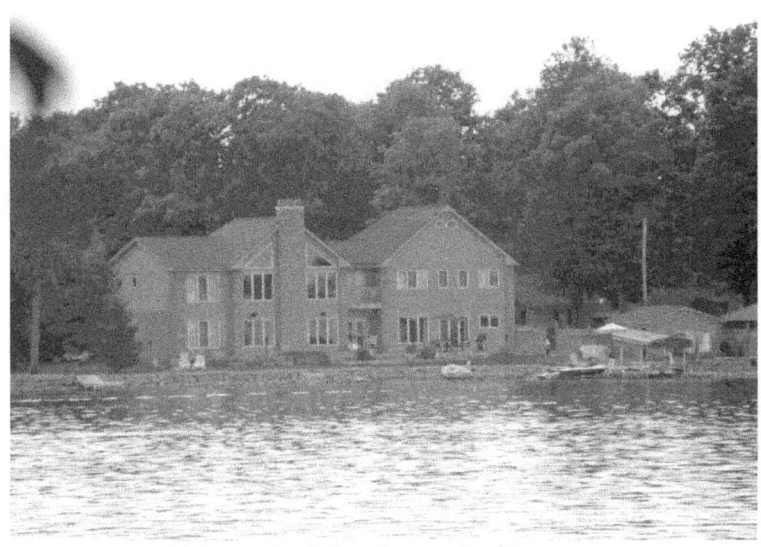

Across the lake from the Burtons

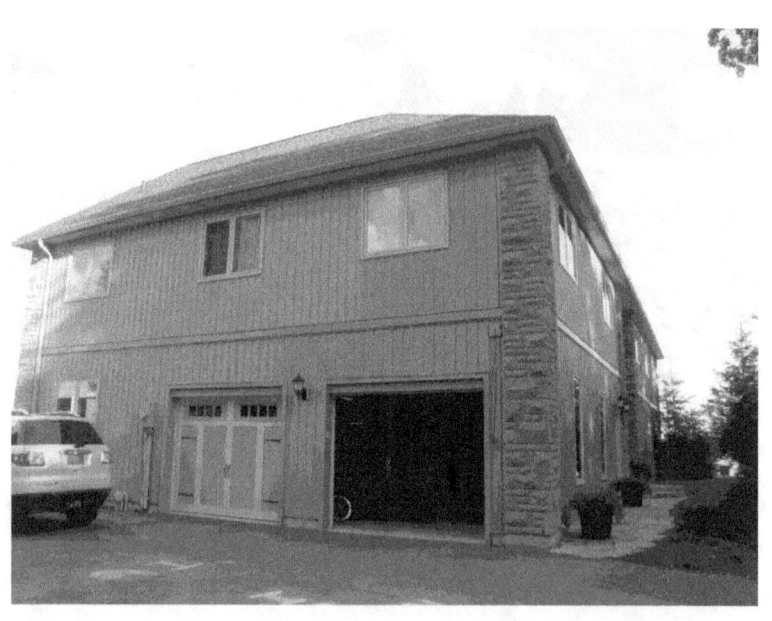

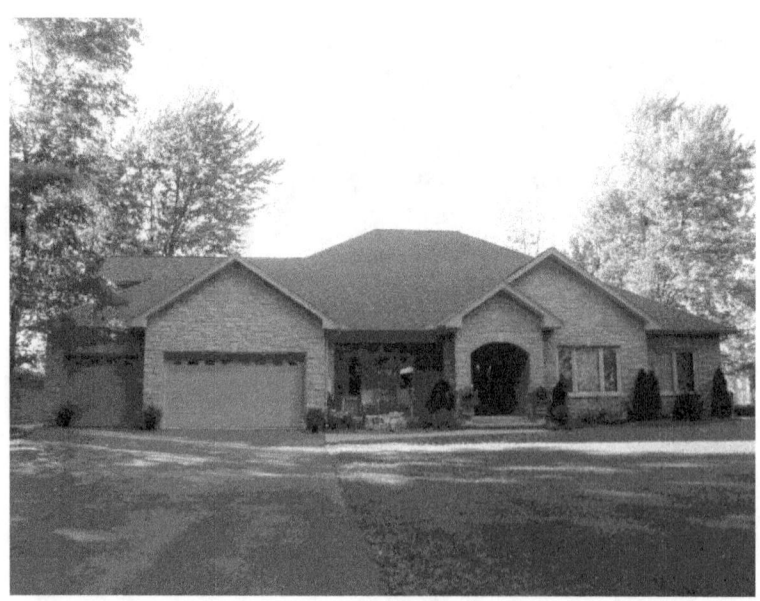

Ennismore

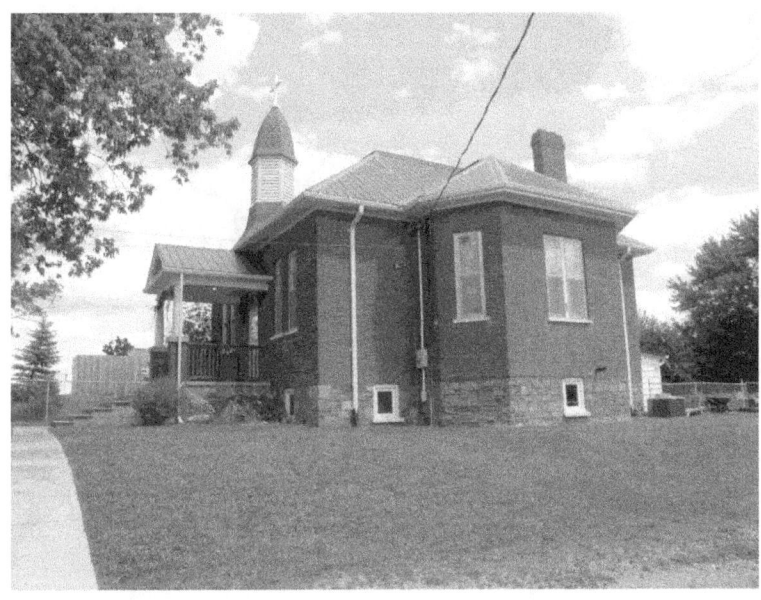

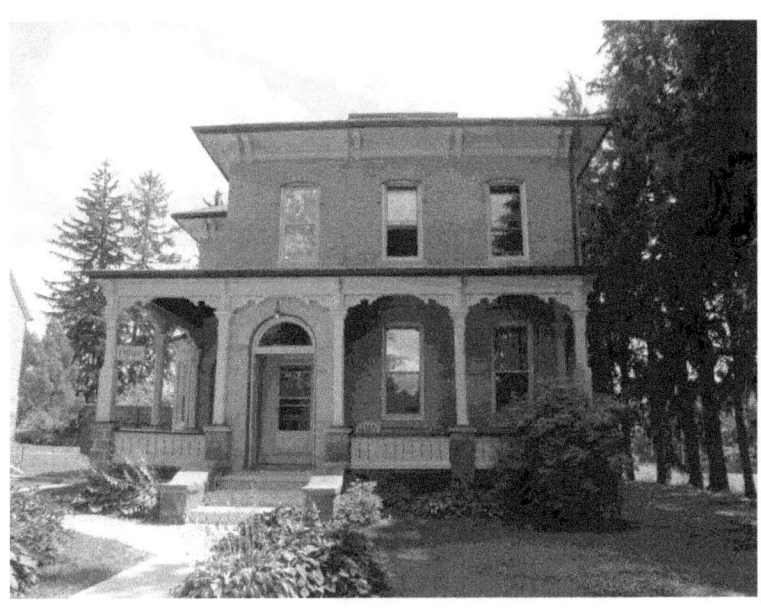

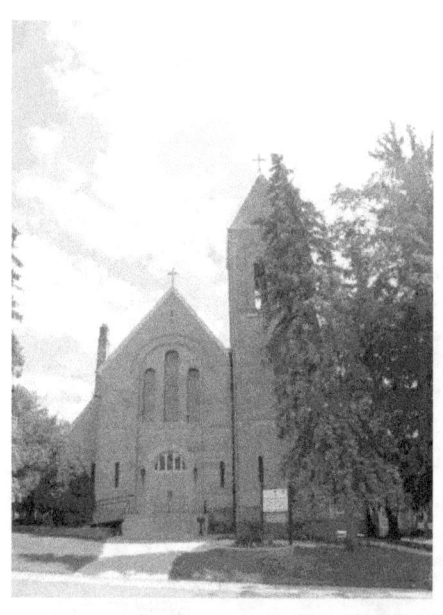

St. Martin of Tours Roman Catholic Parish

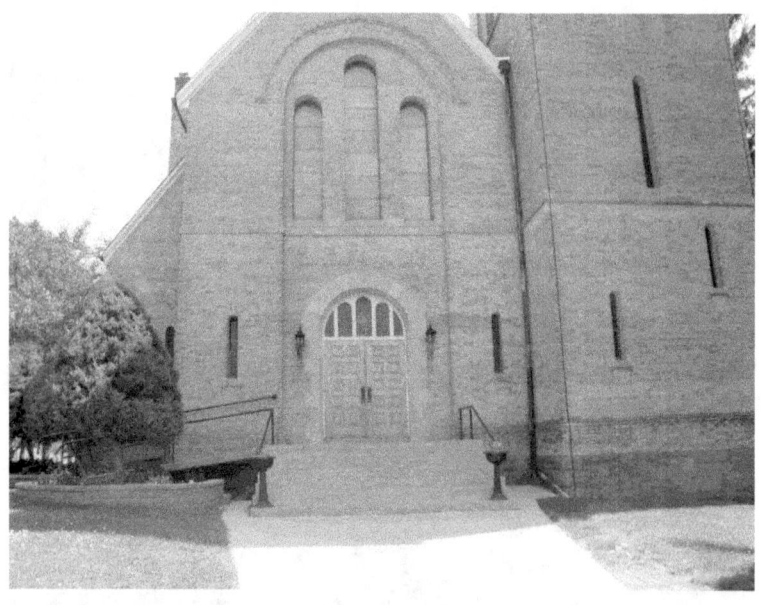

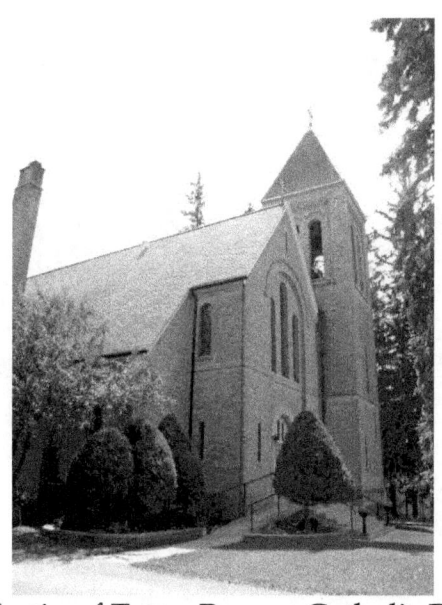

St. Martin of Tours Roman Catholic Parish

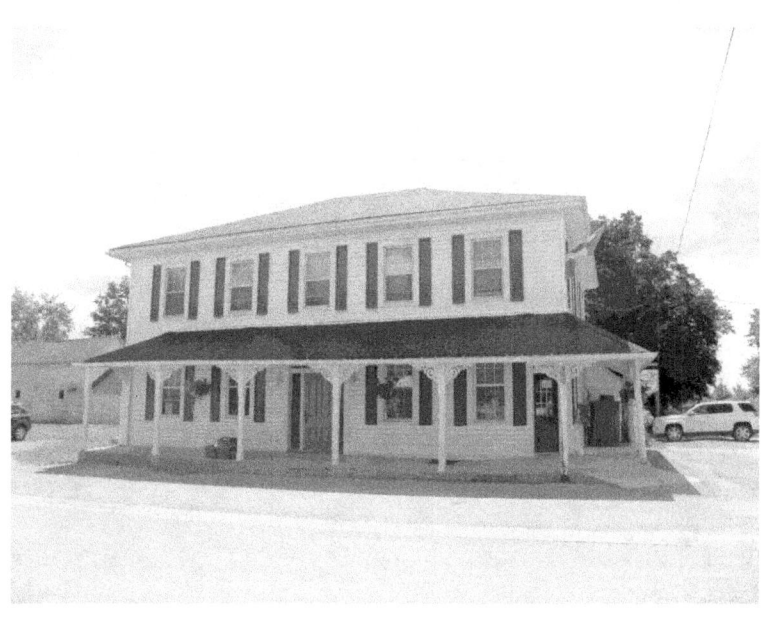

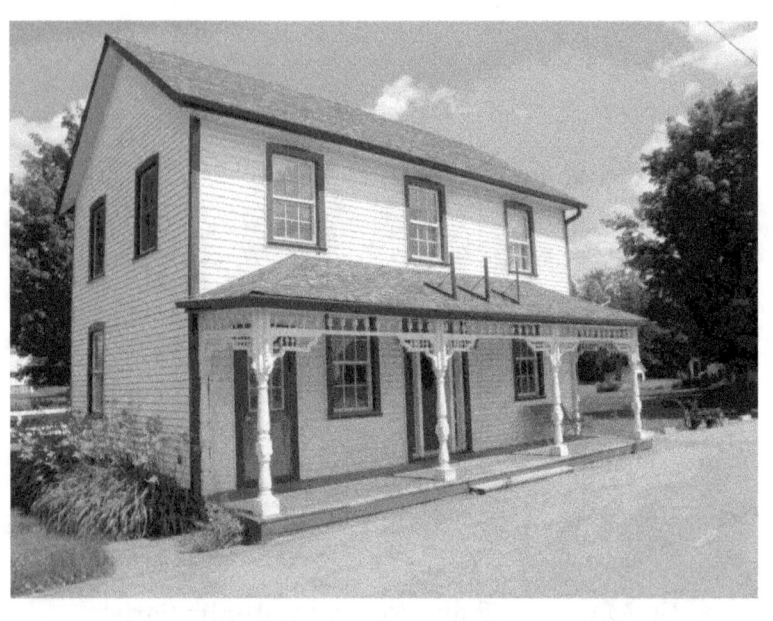

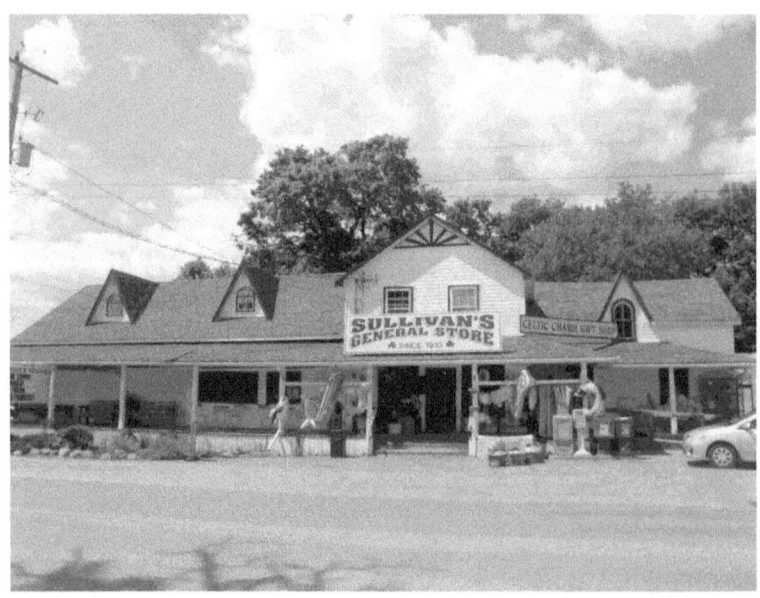

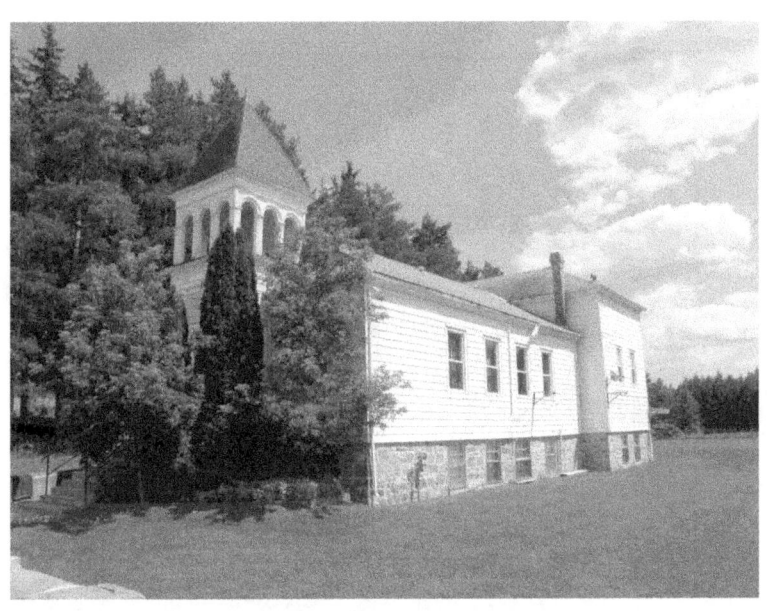

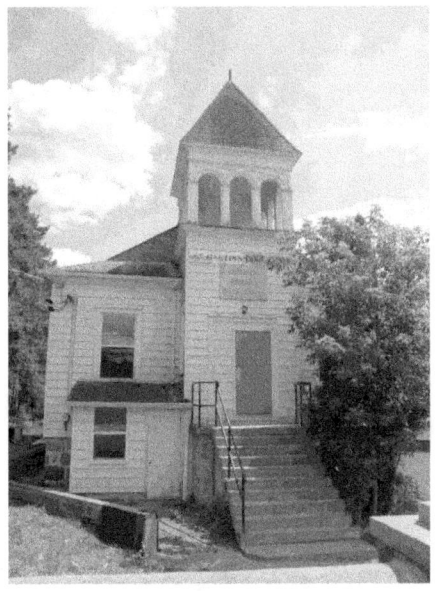

www.ingramcontent.com/pod-product-compliance
Lightning Source LLC
Chambersburg PA
CBHW051343170526
45166CB00002B/930